youth bible studies

Pure Power

FaithWeaver™
Youth Bible Studies

www.faithweaver.com

Group
Loveland, Colorado

Group

FaithWeaver Youth Bible Studies: Pure Power
Copyright © 2000 Group Publishing, Inc.

First Printing, 2000 Edition

Visit our Web site: **www.grouppublishing.com**

Credits

Contributing Authors: Tim Baker, Nancy Going, Jane Vogel, and Paula Meiners Yingst
Editor: Julie Meiklejohn
Creative Development Editor: Karl Leuthauser
Chief Creative Officer: Joani Schultz
Copy Editor: Candace McMahan
Art Director: Jeff Spencer
Cover Art Director: Debbie Collins
Computer Graphic Artist: Fred Schuth
Cover Photography: Cukjati Design
Cover Production Artist: Becky Hawley
Production Manager: Peggy Naylor

ISBN 0-7644-0957-3
Printed in the United States of America.

Contents

Why Do I Need FaithWeaver™ Youth Bible Studies?

A Search Institute study indicates that 86 percent of Christian teenagers do not read the Bible when they are by themselves. There are a variety of reasons, cited in *The Youth Bible*:

"I sometimes don't understand it, so I stop."—Mary in Nebraska

"I'm really confused."—Andrew in Michigan

"I don't know *how* to read the Bible."—Chris in Florida

Part of the reason teenagers find the Bible difficult to understand may be because their exposure to the "whole picture" of God's story has been somewhat limited. Young people often are exposed to the Bible in bits and pieces—a verse here, a passage there—and may never be given instruction about the Bible as a whole—where it came from, how the stories in the Bible fit together, and what the overall meaning of the Bible is. FaithWeaver Youth Bible Studies is designed specifically to help students see the "big picture"— starting with the very beginning of the story of God and his people. Through these studies, your youth will not only begin to see how all of the pieces fit together, they'll also see how the Bible's message is very relevant to their lives today.

Essential Components of FaithWeaver™ Youth Bible Studies

Many elements of FaithWeaver Youth Bible Studies bring exciting benefits to your youth. Here are the highlights:

• **Each study is centered around a Key Question that can be answered through the Bible passage and applied to teenagers' lives.** The Key Question each week leads youth to examine Scripture and discover the answer. Teenagers then examine that answer to determine what relevance it has to them. Before the study is over, teenagers will be challenged to take steps toward active application of that Bible principle, weaving their faith into their lives.

• **Each study teaches to multiple intelligences.** Multiple intelligences describe the different ways in which students are smart. For example, some students may have a great deal of kinesthetic intelligence and learn best using hands-on activities. Other students may have more verbal intelligence; these students learn best by processing things through writing or discussing. Because some of your teenagers may be smart in ways that are different from the ways in which you are smart, resist the impulse to skip activities that don't naturally attract you; they may be just what will resonate with some of your students.

• **Each study provides several adaptation tips for younger or older students.** These tips—containing various age-appropriate options for many of the activities—help you customize each study for the needs of your teenagers.

• **Each study contains an activity to help students explore the historical and cultural context of each Bible story.** The Historical Context box and activity provide valuable Scriptural context information as well as a meaningful way to help students dig a little deeper into the Bible passage.

• **This book comes with a compact disc of great new Christian songs and Music Connection pages.** Each study utilizes these resources to connect with your teenagers through a medium they love—music!

• **Each study includes a "Taking It Home" page.** This page, which you can mail home or distribute during your meeting, provides fun, in-depth activities and discussions to help teenagers explore what they've learned with their families.

• **Each study provides a "Faith Journal" option with a solid assessment question that will help you discover how well your students are learning as well as help you develop better relationships with them.** At the end of each study, you'll be prompted to have students respond to a "sum-up" question on index cards. You'll collect the cards and take some time during the next week to write affirming responses and comments to what they've written. For example, you may write things such as "I'm glad you gained such a knowledge of God's love during this study" or "Hang in there; God is walking beside you. I'm praying for you." Make these comments as personal and meaningful as you can; it will mean a great deal to your students. At the beginning of the next study, you'll be prompted to return the index cards with your comments on them to your students. It's also a good idea to keep copies of the cards in a notebook or a box so that you'll have an ongoing record of how your students are doing.

Some other options for the "Faith Journal" cards might be to have students write any prayer concerns they may have or to have them write their own questions about the topic.

If you notice a student response that seems troubling, be sure to touch base with the student sometime right before or after your next meeting. If a student seems to be having problems you're not comfortable handling, ask your pastor or your Christian education director for help.

These innovative, effective learning techniques will transform your classroom into a relational, fun, and caring place for learning. FaithWeaver Youth Bible Studies will help you change the lives of your teenagers and ensure that authentic learning takes place.

About Your Students

FaithWeaver Youth Bible Studies was written and developed by people who have significant experience working with teenagers. We've designed the studies to be interesting, beneficial, and age-appropriate for youth. As you use the studies to encourage their faith and growth, you might want to keep the following in mind:

• Teenagers' spirituality is, above all, **personal**. They are ready to embrace a more personal relationship with Christ.

• Teenagers' spirituality is **relational**. Relationships with family, friends, peers, and teachers are of high importance to teenagers; they can be encouraged and challenged to examine those relationships in the light of a personal relationship with Christ.

• Teenagers' spirituality is beginning to focus on **future living**. As teenagers look toward their futures, they can be encouraged to consider how their current choices can create their responses to Christ's call in the future.

• Teenagers' spirituality is **multifaceted**. Teenagers hope to discover how their faith can touch and be reflected in all aspects of their lives.

• Teenagers' spirituality is affected by their **physical and mental development**. As their brains develop and their bodies change, teenagers' capacity to think undergoes a dramatic shift, and their worlds broaden. They become more capable of thinking cognitively and metaphorically.

There's More...

FaithWeaver Youth Bible Studies is just one of the components of Group's FaithWeaver™ family of Christian growth resources. This system of resources is composed of three major elements and other supporting materials. The major elements are FaithWeaver Bible Curriculum, FaithWeaver Children's Church, and FaithWeaver Midweek. Supporting materials include HomeConnect resources for families and PastorConnect resources for pastors. Any one of the elements below can be used without the others. However, using all of them together will help your church's families learn and grow in faith both at church and at home in a way no single book can.

• **FaithWeaver Bible Curriculum**—Designed for use in Sunday school, this portion of the system concentrates on education. Infants through adults cover the same Bible story, learning about it and applying it at appropriate levels for all age groupings. When you use FaithWeaver Youth Bible Studies, you can tie teenagers into a bigger picture of all-church learning.

• **FaithWeaver Children's Church**—This program includes both preschool and elementary children, with options for joint and separate activities for each. The focus of this element is to learn about worship and to practice it together, while connecting with the story or topic covered in FaithWeaver Bible Curriculum. Here's an opportunity for teenagers to help lead and support children.

• **FaithWeaver Midweek**—Still in development, this program focuses on relationships and service, giving children opportunities to demonstrate their faith in their lives. This will be another leadership opportunity for teenagers to mentor younger children.

• **FaithWeaver HomeConnect**™—Two significant resources to help weave faith into life at home are the Adult FaithWeaver Bible Curriculum and the Driving Home the Point weekly page. Within the adult curriculum, a segment written especially for parents and caregivers gives them ways to continue the faith development of their children at home. And the Driving Home the Point weekly pages contain devotions, discussions, extra activities, and suggestions to keep the family growing in faith together after leaving the church building.

• **FaithWeaver PastorConnect**™—This element also contains two resources. The first is The Pastor Handbook, which helps the pastor know what's going on in the education program. Using it, the pastor can choose to connect messages or church services with what's being taught. The second resource is a yearly book of children's sermons, *FaithWeaver Children's Messages*, that allows the pastor to present a children's sermon each week that supplements what children are studying in Sunday school.

• **FaithWeaver Internet Link**—Please visit our Web site at www.faith-weaver.com to download FaithWeaver materials or to obtain more information about the system.

You're Important to Jesus!

 1

Jesus Blesses the Children

 key question: How do you know you are important to Jesus?

study focus: Teenagers will discover that Jesus values those who receive him with childlike faith.

Key Verse:
"Let the little children come to me, and do not hinder them, for the kingdom of God belongs to such as these" (MARK 10:14b).

A Look at the Study

Study Sequence	Minutes	What Students Will Do	Classroom Supplies
Getting Started	5 to 10	**Feeling Important**—Recall ways people made them feel important when they were children.	
Bible Story Exploration	10 to 15	**Fame**—Compare a celebrity's reaction to fame to Jesus' reaction.	Bibles, photocopies of "Historical Context" box (p. 11), pens
	15 to 20	**VIC—Very Important Children**—Express the emotions children might have felt when the disciples denied them and when Jesus received them.	Bibles, pens, "VIC—Very Important Children" handouts (p. 16), crayons
Bible Application	15 to 20	**Like a Child**—Consider scenarios from the perspective of a little child.	
	up to 5	**Faith Journal**—Respond in writing to the Key Question.	Index cards, pens
Music Connection	10 to 15	**I Will Rest in You**—Create an outline and description of the perfect father to better understand God as the perfect Father. Use this option at an appropriate time in the study.	CD: "I Will Rest in You" (Track 1), CD player, newsprint, markers

Age-Level Insight

Teenagers are looking for their place in the world. They need more than the knowledge that they'll be successful or have friends. They're asking deeper questions. They want to know who *really* loves them. They long to feel and to know that they're important—that importance tells them they're OK. As you teach this lesson to your students, be sure to make the message of the lesson specific. In other words, don't just say, "Everyone is important to God." Rather, look each individual in the eye and say, "You are important to God!"

Getting Started

Feeling Important

Ask students to think about a time in their childhood when someone made them feel valued or special. Invite each person to share his or her story, telling specifically what the person did that communicated value. For example, one student may remember a Sunday school teacher who gave her a hug each week. Another might tell about a neighbor who made him feel capable by letting him "help" in the garden, even though it would have been easier for the neighbor to work alone.

ASK • How did people communicate to you that you were important when you were a child?

• How did it feel to know you were important to the person you told us about?

• Do you think you're important to Jesus? Why or why not?

• If you know you're important to Jesus, how does that make you feel?

Bible Story Exploration

Fame

Give each student a Bible, a copy of the "Historical Context" box (p. 11), and a pen. Ask teenagers to read the Scripture passage listed on the handout.

ASK • Who is the most famous and popular person alive today?

• What would it take for you to see that person? to talk to the person? to hug the person?

SAY Find a partner. Draw a line down the middle of the back of your handout. On the left side of the handout, list the things that most famous people value. After you complete your list, make a list of the things Jesus values.

ASK • What are some differences between the way Jesus dealt with popularity and the way people deal with it today?

• Why aren't you important to most famous people?

• How do you know you're important to Jesus?

VIC—Very Important Children

Give each student a Bible, a "VIC—Very Important Children" handout (p. 16), and a pen. Make crayons available to the whole group.

SAY Read Mark 10:13-16 again. Then imagine that you were one of the children in this story. How did you feel when the disciples tried to send you away? How did you feel when Jesus called you to him? Illustrate your emotions by drawing a picture on the paper or by writing a childlike song about your feelings. I'd really like you to try to remember what it was like to be a child. So enter into the mind of a ten-year-old as you create your presentation.

Historical Context | Mark 10:13-16

Imagine a celebrity today on his way to a big movie premiere. Surrounded by "handlers," he hurries from his car into the theater, basking in the admiration of fans but not stopping to give anyone special attention. This may be the picture the disciples had of Jesus. They saw it as their job to keep the masses away from Jesus—especially those as insignificant as children. After all, he was a very important spiritual leader, and he needed all his strength and emotional energy to fight off the attacks of the Pharisees. He needed to be spending his time with those who were influential and powerful. He certainly shouldn't be wasting his time with small children.

But as he did many times in his ministry, Jesus challenged the status quo. He ignored what the disciples considered politically important—appeasing the religious leaders of the day—and spent his time blessing children. He knew that the Pharisees' hearts were set against him. They didn't want to learn from him or follow him; they just wanted to lure him into one of their traps (Mark 10:2). So he turned his attention to those with tender hearts: the children (and their parents!).

The parents had come to Jesus seeking a blessing on their children from this great teacher. It's easy for us to picture Jesus laying his hand on a child's head and giving a few words of blessing. But he did more than that; he took the children in his arms and hugged them! And then he blessed them.

Think about it. If you were a parent of one of these small children whom the famous Jesus of Nazareth stopped to bless, what would *you* think of Jesus? How would you respond later when you heard he'd been crucified and then rose from the dead? If you were one of the children, think about all the times you'd be told the story of being held and blessed by Jesus! In this act of blessing the children, Jesus showed the common person—even the small child—how important we all are to him.

Another theme also winds through this passage: To make it to heaven, you must become like one of these small children. What did Jesus mean by that? What makes one fit for God's kingdom? The religious leaders had it all wrong. As the church sometimes does today, they relegated children to a place of insignificance until they grew to adulthood. Instead, we must value and encourage the qualities of children that make them receptive to the grace Jesus offers.

What are the qualities of children that make them well-suited for God's kingdom? They're humble and trusting, which prepares them to naturally put their faith in Jesus. Jesus' message is that, just as children place their trust in their parents, we must be humble and willing to place our trust in God. We can't work our way into heaven through all the right actions, as the Pharisees tried to do. We must relax and trust Jesus, as these small children did.

Your students are important to God, regardless of their age or influence. Help them see the mercy and grace God offers in Jesus to every person everywhere.

How many of the teenagers in your group carry pagers? have cell phones? have part-time jobs? The world is a hectic and busy place for teenagers. As a leader, you are responsible for challenging their thinking and encouraging their understanding of God by providing opportunities for serious and in-depth Bible study and character development. However, it's just as important to give teenagers an opportunity to let down their guard and play. Encourage teenagers to enjoy and wonder at the experience of being young. Help them see that they will soon be adults with even more responsibility and that it's a waste for them to spend their adolescence focused only on becoming adults.

Tip From
the Trenches

Repeating the Key Verse in this way will not only demonstrate its importance; it will also help your students begin to memorize it.

Allow students about five minutes to work. Ask a student to read Mark 10:13-16 aloud. Then ask volunteers to present their illustrations and songs. After the first volunteer shares, point out the Key Verse on the handout.

SAY After each person shares a picture or song, we'll all read this verse aloud.

ASK • How did Jesus show that the children were important to him?

• How do you know that you're important to Jesus?

Bible Application

Like a Child

ASK • What does it mean to "receive the kingdom of God like a little child"?

Have teenagers form groups of four.

SAY To help you understand what Jesus is asking of us, I'd like you to try to adopt the mind-set of a little child. With your group, think about how a preschooler would react to each of the situations I read to you. After you've talked about the preschooler's reaction to each situation, discuss why you think a child that age would act that way.

Give groups an opportunity to discuss each of the following situations, and take a moment between each discussion to allow groups to share their insights with the entire class:

• Madison's parents believe that God created the world in six literal days and have taught Madison accordingly. In her third day of preschool, Madison's teacher had all of the children pretend to be monkeys while explaining that people come from monkeys. When Madison exclaimed to the teacher that God created the world, her teacher remarked that most people don't really believe that anymore. How do you think Madison would react? What would she tell her parents? Who would she believe? Why?

• Marcus was playing on the slide at the park while his dad sat nearby reading a book. Marcus went down the slide a little too fast and did a face-plant in the sand. What would Marcus do? Why?

• Teresa has always been a little frightened of the dark. Teresa's mom told her that she doesn't have to be afraid because God is with her in the room. Would Teresa believe her mom? Why or why not?

After you've discussed all three situations,

ASK • What are some characteristics of little children?

- What does this say about what it means to "receive the kingdom of God like a little child"?

- How can you "receive the kingdom of God like a little child" on a daily basis?

- Why are children so important to God?

- Why are people so important to God?

- How do you know you're important to God?

SAY Perhaps Jesus calls us to receive his kingdom as little children because he wants us to be dependent on him for our needs, to be humble, and to trust in him. God cares for you so much, and he wants you to lean on and trust in his provision like a little child. I'd like you to take a few minutes to ask God to help you to be more childlike in your faith.

Have students disperse around the room and spend a few minutes in silent prayer, asking God to help them depend on him, walk in humility, trust in him, and receive the kingdom as little children. Encourage your teenagers to ask for help in specific areas where they don't have childlike faith.

for OLDER teenagers

Older teenagers may discover characteristics of young children (such as self-centeredness) that confuse Jesus' metaphor about how we should accept the kingdom of God. Consider sharing this chart with your students and discussing the differences between childish and childlike faith.

"Childish" Faith	"Childlike" Faith
• Good Christians don't have pain and disappointments	• God uses our pain and disappointment to make us better Christians
• God helps those who help themselves	• God can only begin to help those who admit their own helplessness
• God wants to make us happy	• God wants to make us holy
• God always answers prayers	• Sometimes he answers with "No" or "Wait"
• Faith will help us to always understand what God is doing	• Faith will help us to stand under God's sovereignty even when we don't have a clue about what God is doing
• The closer we get to God, the more perfect we become	• The closer we get to God, the more we become aware of our own sinfulness
• Mature Christians have all the answers	• Mature Christians can wrestle honestly with tough questions because we trust that God has the answers
• Good Christians are always strong	• Our strength is in admitting our weakness

Source: Duffy Robbins, "Faith: Childish or Childlike?" Good News, March/April 1996

Faith Journal

Give each student an index card and a pen. Have teenagers write their answers to the following question on their index cards:

• **How do you know you're important to Jesus?**

After teenagers have written their responses, ask them to return the cards to you. Before you meet with the group again, take time to write personal responses to your students on their index cards. You may want to keep a notebook or a box containing copies of these index cards as well as brief notes of prayer concerns and needs your students share using this assessment tool.

For further information about the Faith Journal option, refer to page 5 of the Introduction.

Music Connection

idea:listen

[music]

Have teenagers form groups of four. Give each group a sheet of newsprint and a marker. Have each group draw an outline of a person.

SAY **God describes himself in the Bible as the perfect Father. With your group, I'd like you to describe a perfect father by labeling different parts of the outline you just drew. For example, you could write "strong and tender arms" on the outline's arms or "big heart" on the chest of the outline.**

Give groups about five minutes to work. Then allow each group to present its outline.

SAY **I'm going to play a song called "I Will Rest in You" by Jaci Velasquez. As you listen to the song, think about what it's like to be before God like a little child.**

 Track 1
Play "I Will Rest in You" by Jaci Velasquez.

ASK • **What does it mean to approach God like a little child?**

   • **Do you feel comfortable coming before God like a child? Why or why not?**

   • **What comfort do you find in the fact that God truly is the perfect Father?**

I Will Rest in You

(recorded by Jaci Velasquez)

Lord, I'm in the dark,
Seems to me the line is dead when I come calling.
No one there; the sky is falling.
Lord I need to know—
My mind is playing games again—
You're right where you have always been.

Take me back to you,
The place that I once knew as a little child.
Constantly the eyes of God watched over me.
Oh, I want to be in the place that I once knew as
     a little child,
Fall into the bed of faith prepared for me.
I will rest in you.

Tell me I'm a fool.
Tell me that you love me for the fool I am,
And comfort me like only you can.
And tell me there's a place
Where I can feel your breath
Like sweet caresses on my face again.

[think]

Read Mark 10:13.

Imagine that you were one of the children in this story. How would you have felt when the disciples tried to send you away? Use this space to illustrate those emotions. Or, instead of drawing, create a childlike song to express the emotions.

Now read Mark 10:14-16.

How did you feel when Jesus called you to him? Express your response to Jesus' actions by creating another illustration or childlike tune.

*research
required*

OK
to copy

> ### KEY VERSE
> "Let the little children come to me, and do not hinder them, for the kingdom of God belongs to such as these" (MARK 10:14b).

Driving Home the Point:

everywhere

In Dr. Seuss' classic book **Horton Hears a Who!**, Horton the elephant valiantly strives to protect a microscopic population from animals who refuse to believe that a person's a person, no matter how small. Here's how the story ends:

Finally, at last! From that speck on that clover

Their voices were heard! They rang out clear and clean.

And the elephant smiled. "Do you see what I mean?...

They've proved they ARE persons, no matter how small.

And their whole world was saved by the Smallest of All!"

"How true! Yes, how true," said the big kangaroo.

"And, from now on, you know what I'm planning to do?...

From now on, I'm going to protect them with you!"

And the young kangaroo in her pouch said,...

"... ME, TOO!

From sun in the summer. From rain when it's fall-ish,

I'm going to protect them. No matter how small-ish!"

Talking At Home:

Read Psalm 8 with your family, and discuss these questions:

• **What does this passage tell us about how God views human beings?**

• **How can we respond to the position God has given us?**

Ask each family member to think of a time he or she learned something "from the lips of children and infants" or from someone who seemed unimportant. Talk about why God chooses to use people who appear weak or insignificant.

Mercy!

Mark 10:46-52

Jesus Heals a Blind Man

 key question: How does Jesus show he cares for us?

 study focus: Teenagers will recognize Jesus' mercy in the life of a biblical character and in their own lives.

Key Verse:
"He saved us, not because of righteous things we had done, but because of his mercy" (Titus 3:5a).

A Look at the Study

Study Sequence	Minutes	What Students Will Do	Classroom Supplies
Getting Started	10 to 15	**Before and After**—Rewrite a stanza of "Amazing Grace."	Paper, pens, newsprint, marker
Bible Story Exploration	10 to 15	**In Need**—Identify and pray for their spiritual and emotional needs.	Bibles, photocopies of "Historical Context" box (p. 21)
	25 to 30	**Man-on-the-Street Interviews**—Retell the story of Bartimaeus as newscast interviewers.	Bibles, "Terms of Endearment" handouts (p. 25), pens
Bible Application	15 to 20	**Mercy to Me**—Explore the meaning of mercy and offer a prayer in response to God's merciful salvation.	"Terms of Endearment" handouts (pp. 25-27), pens
	up to 5	**Faith Journal**—Respond in writing to the Key Question.	Index cards, pens
Music Connection	10 to 15	**The Only Thing I Need**—Compile a list of all that God has given them to emphasize how God has cared for them. Use this option at an appropriate time in the study.	CD: "The Only Thing I Need" (Track 2), CD player, tape, newsprint, markers

Age-Level Insight

Everyone needs to feel cared for. Many teenagers are left to raise themselves through choices they have made or those their parents have made. In these difficult circumstances, teenagers' developmental need to be cared for intensifies. Many of them have a hard time understanding how an "invisible" God could care for them. As you explore this study with your group, remember that these young people are looking for tangible ways to know that God is concerned about them.

Last Week's Impact

As teenagers arrive, greet them warmly, and ask follow-up questions to review last week's study and Key Verse. Ask questions such as "What kinds of things have you experienced that show you your importance to Jesus?" and "What did your family members share about why God chooses to use those who seem weak or insignificant?"

If you used the Faith Journal option last week, take this time to return your students' index cards to them.

Tip From the Trenches

If your students are very comfortable with one another, ask each pair to sing its own stanza. If you think this will be intimidating for some students, either sing all the stanzas as a group or invite some performance-oriented volunteers to sing all the stanzas for the group.

Getting Started

Before and After

Ask volunteers to share brief stories about times they were lost—physically, spiritually, or emotionally—and how it felt to be found again. Then ask how many students know the hymn "Amazing Grace." Remind students of the words of the first stanza:

> Amazing grace—how sweet the sound—
> That saved a wretch like me!
> I once was lost but now am found,
> Was blind but now I see.

ASK • **Can you identify with this stanza? Explain.**

• **What feelings does it bring to mind?**

Ask students to form pairs. Give pairs paper and pens, and ask them to rewrite the last two lines of the stanza using before-and-after metaphors that reflect their own experiences. Challenge pairs to write their lines so that they can be sung to the tune of "Amazing Grace." For example, a pair might write:

> Amazing grace—how sweet the sound—
> That saved a wretch like me!
> I once was broke but now have cash,
> Was flunking but now have a B.

When the pairs have finished, collect the songs, write them on newsprint, and sing them together.

ASK • **What do you think the before-and-after metaphors in the original hymn are trying to communicate about God?**

• **What are some ways God shows he cares for us?**

SAY **Today we're going to read about a man who could have identified with the hymn "Amazing Grace" very well—he was a man who was blind and then could see.**

Bible Story Exploration

In Need

Give each student a Bible and a copy of the "Historical Context" box (p. 21). Have teenagers read the Scripture passage and the handout. Then have the class form trios to discuss these questions:

ASK • **What were Bartimaeus' needs?**

• **What are your emotional and spiritual needs?**

• **Why do you think God wants us to ask for help when he knows what we need anyway?**

SAY Take some time in your trios to pray for the emotional and spiritual needs you discussed. Make sure your trio prays for each person.

Give groups a few minutes to pray.

SAY Jesus cared for Bartimaeus, and he cares deeply for you. You can be confident that Jesus will help you with your needs when you ask him, just as he helped Bartimaeus.

Historical Context | Mark 10:46-52

Leaving Jericho on his way to Jerusalem, Jesus had gathered a crowd. Bartimaeus' blindness didn't prevent him from hearing the ruckus of the approaching crowd and from asking who was creating all the fuss. When he found out, his cries of "Son of David" in addressing Jesus were not just a way of identifying Jesus' lineage. Since the term "Son of David" is clearly a reference to the Messiah, Bartimaeus was shouting to both the crowd and to Jesus that he believed Jesus was the promised Messiah. Also, his persistence, even when people tried to hush him, showed that he was convinced Jesus could heal his blindness.

Matthew's and Luke's versions of this event differ slightly from Mark's. Matthew says two blind men were healed, while Luke suggests Jesus was entering Jericho instead of leaving it. Both of these seeming discrepancies have understandable explanations. First, though Mark and Luke tell of the healing of only one man, that doesn't mean there couldn't have been another. Certainly Jesus did many things that were not reported. And from Luke 19, we see that Jesus had passed through Jericho when he met Zacchaeus then returned to Jericho with him for dinner. So it is likely just a matter of perspective whether Jesus was leaving Jericho or entering it when he healed Bartimaeus.

Although Jesus was surrounded by a crowd and was set on reaching his destination, his ears and heart were attuned to the cry of one calling out for mercy. Perhaps some of the people around him were just interested in following a celebrity. Others may simply have been curious about Jesus. But Bartimaeus needed Jesus' mercy, and Jesus heard his cry.

In acknowledging Bartimaeus' identification of him as the Son of David, Jesus was also making a statement. Earlier in his ministry he had avoided being identified as the Messiah. But now, as he was making his last trip to Jerusalem, where he would be crucified, he was ready for his identity to be known. And what better way to make that announcement than to heal someone who had faith in him!

It's interesting to note that Jesus didn't force any agenda on Bartimaeus. He asked what Bartimaeus wanted. We can learn a lesson from that: Although God is in control of all the resources in the universe, he wants us to express our needs to him. He wants us to acknowledge our dependence upon him and seek his mercy, which he generously bestows on us.

Notice also that Bartimaeus' faith in Jesus initiated his healing. Jesus didn't say, "Because you've lived a good life in spite of your hardship, I'll heal you." He didn't say, "Because your parents were so faithful to me, I'll give you your sight." Jesus responded to Bartimaeus' faith. Things haven't changed: Jesus responds to our needs on the basis of our faith, not because of anything good we've done or any specific set of words we repeat. Jesus shows us he cares for us by taking care of our needs as we acknowledge our dependence on him and trust in him to meet those needs. And what Jesus asks in return is that we do as Bartimaeus did and follow Jesus along the roads of our lives, no matter how old or young we may be!

Man-on-the-Street Interviews

Form at least three teams of two to four people per team. Distribute Bibles, pens, and the "Terms of Endearment" handout (pp. 25-27).

SAY **The event we're going to study today would have made a terrific news story. In your news team, you're going to prepare a portion of a "live" interview for the Jericho Nightly News.**

Assign each team one of the casts of characters on the handout: Jesus and his disciples; Bartimaeus and his friends; and bystanders.

SAY **Together, read Mark 10:46-52 again, the terms defined on your handout, and the Key Verse on your handout. Next, answer the questions for your characters. Then choose one person on your news team to be the interviewer, and have the rest play the parts of the characters listed. Be ready to present your interview in about eight minutes.**

When the teams are ready, play the part of a news anchorperson, and

SAY **Good evening, ladies and gentlemen. This is the Jericho Nightly News. An amazing event happened today just outside the walls of our fair city. For an eyewitness account, we go live to** [student's name].

Have each news team present its interview.

After all the teams have made their presentations, discuss the questions listed on the handout.

SAY **We've seen how Jesus showed that he cared about Bartimaeus.**

ASK • **How does Jesus show he cares for us?**

Bible Application

Mercy to Me

Make sure everyone still has a copy of the "Terms of Endearment" handout (pp. 25-27). Direct students to the Key Verse. Have students discuss the following questions in their news teams and then report back to the whole group after each question.

• **How does this Key Verse relate to the story we've been studying?**

• **Bartimaeus asked Jesus to show mercy. How did Jesus' responses to Bartimaeus fit the definition of mercy written on your handout?**

• **Since Jesus said that Bartimaeus' faith had healed him, does that mean that Bartimaeus deserved to be healed? How does that fit with the definition of mercy?**

ASK • **In what ways besides physical healing does God show mercy?**

• **In what ways has God shown mercy to you?** ⁇

If students don't mention it themselves, direct them to the Key Verse and remind them that God's greatest act of mercy is the gift of salvation.

Distribute pens. Have students look again at the Key Verse on the handout and then rewrite it to personalize it. Suggest that they incorporate the definition of mercy and that they use specific examples of "righteous things" they may have done that cannot earn them salvation. For instance, someone might write, "Jesus saved me, Michael, not because my parents are Christians or because I come to Sunday school or because I'm a nice guy, but because he chose to show compassion and kindness to me instead of severity, even though I don't deserve it."

When everyone has finished, form a circle. Invite volunteers to read their restatements of the verse aloud as a prayer, addressing them to Jesus: "Thank you, Jesus, that you saved me..." Don't force anyone to say this prayer aloud. Some may not know Christ as their Savior. Instead invite interested students to come to you afterward and talk about Jesus.

Faith Journal

Give each student an index card and a pen. Have teenagers write their answers to the following question on their index cards:

• **How has God shown you that he cares for you?** ⁇

After teenagers have written their responses, ask them to return the cards to you. Before you meet with the group again, take time to write personal responses to your students on their index cards. You may want to keep a notebook or a box containing copies of these index cards as well as brief notes of prayer concerns and needs your students share using this assessment tool.

For further information about the Faith Journal option, refer to page 5 of the Introduction.

For further information about the Faith Journal option, refer to page 5 of the Introduction.

For Extra Impact

Heighten the illusion of a newscast by videotaping the interviews and then playing them sequentially for the students to watch.

for OLDER teenagers

Although Jesus simply told Bartimaeus, "Go," the Bible tells us that Bartimaeus "followed Jesus" (Mark 10:52). Older teenagers may like to discuss Bartimaeus' response as a pattern for their own response to Jesus' acts of mercy in their lives, exploring what it means for them to follow Jesus.

Tip From the Trenches

To help strengthen the connection between church and home, photocopy the "Taking It Home" page at the end of this study, and either distribute copies to students before they leave or mail them to their homes. Encourage students to complete the reading, activities, and discussion with their families during the coming week.

Tape a large sheet of newsprint to a wall, and set markers near it.

SAY **Take a minute or two to think about all that God has given you. Try to determine which three of the things God has given you are the most important in your life.**

After a minute or two, have each teenager list the three items on the sheet of newsprint.

SAY **God has given us so much. I'm going to play a song by 4Him with Jon Anderson. As you listen to the song, think about how God has taken care of you.**

 Track 2
Play the song. When it's over,

ASK • **What does the song say about how God takes care of you?**

• **What does the list on the newsprint say about how God takes care of us?**

• **How has God taken care of you?**

The Only Thing I Need

(recorded by 4Him with Jon Anderson)

*Eyes closed in a veil of tears when I hear the
    sound,
Once more you've come to me—you've calmed me
    down.
You still the raging sea inside of me.
My Lord has come for me.*

*Why...why is it so hard for me to see?
Why is it so hard to just believe?
Show me what it means to be free.*

*The only thing I need I already have,
The fullness of your mercy in my hand,
The only One who loves me as I am.
The only thing I need I already have.*

*My heart—a companion to my wounded soul.
Again you comfort me...you take control.
You quell the fear that owns too much of me,
As it was meant to be.*

*So why...when each and every word becomes a
    war,
When there's nothing I can see worth fighting for,*

You come into my heart and set me free?

*You're all I need...already have it.
All I need...already have it.*

From the album *Streams*. Words and music by Brent Bourgeois. Copyright © 1999 Wordspring Music, Inc./ADC Music (administered by Wordspring Music, Inc.)/SESAC. All rights reserved. Used by permission.

- **Son of David**—"a name the Jews used for the Christ because the Savior was to come from the family of King David" *(The Youth Bible)*

- **Mercy**—"Compassion or kindness shown to someone instead of severity, especially to someone who doesn't deserve it" *(The Quest Study Bible)*

- **Faith**—"Now faith is being sure of what we hope for and certain of what we do not see" (Hebrews 11:1).

In your news team, read Mark 10:46-52 and Titus 3:5a (printed on page 27). Use the definitions above to deepen your understanding of the passages. Then work as a team to answer the questions for your cast of characters.

When you've answered the questions for your cast of characters, use them to prepare a list of questions for your interviewer to ask the rest of the cast. Be sure to give everyone on your news team a chance to talk during the interview.

Jesus and His Disciples

Cast: Interviewer, Jesus, Disciples (optional)

- **If you had been one of the disciples, how would you have expected Jesus to respond to the blind man? Why?**

_____

_____

- **Why do you think Jesus called the blind man?**

_____

_____

- **Why did Jesus ask Bartimaeus what he wanted? Didn't Jesus already know?**

_____

_____

- **Why did Jesus heal Bartimaeus?**

_____

_____

- **What did Jesus mean when he said, "Your faith has healed you"?**

_____

_____

- **What did you learn about Jesus from this event?**

_____

_____

research required

[t h i n k]

• How does Jesus show he cares for us?

Bartimaeus and His Friends

Cast: Interviewer, Bartimaeus, Friends (optional)

• What did Bartimaeus mean when he called Jesus "Son of David"?

• What does that tell you about Bartimaeus?

• What else can you learn about Bartimaeus from his words and actions?

• Imagine you are one of Bartimaeus' friends. What would your reaction be to his bold request?

• Jesus said that Bartimaeus had faith. How was that faith evident?

• What do you think Bartimaeus did after he gained his sight?

• What qualities of Bartimaeus would you like to have in your own life?

• How does Jesus show he cares for us?

Bystanders

Cast: Interviewer, Bystanders

[think]

• **Why do you think the bystanders told Bartimaeus to be quiet?**

_____

_____

• **What does that tell you about their understanding of Jesus and his ministry?**

_____

_____

• **What do you think the crowd's reaction was when Jesus healed Bartimaeus? (Read Luke 18:35–43 for another telling of the event.) Why?**

_____

_____

• **How do you think the bystanders would have described Jesus after this event?**

_____

_____

• **How does Jesus show he cares for us?**

_____

_____

research required

> ### KEY VERSE
> "He saved us, not because of righteous things we had done, but because of his mercy" (Titus 3:5a).

Taking It Home

Talking About It

take home! *everywhere*

Driving Home the Point:

When Ben Strong and Michael Carneal arrived at school on that Monday morning more than a year ago, both of them knew exactly what they wanted to do.

So at 7:37 a.m. on December 1, 1997, Ben and about thirty-five other students gathered...holding hands, singing songs, and talking to God.

As soon as the students said, "Amen," Michael pulled out a pistol and started shooting.

Three girls died in the attack—Nicole [Hadley], fifteen-year-old Kayce Steger, and seventeen-year-old Jessica James. Five other students were injured, including Missy Jenkins who is paralyzed from the chest down.

Ben says he forgave Michael "immediately."

Ben's not the only student to have forgiven Michael. Many others have publicly stated their forgiveness. Within days of the shooting, some of them had put up a huge banner in the [school] hallways that read, "We forgive you, Mike!"

None of the students has spoken with Michael since the shooting, but several, including Ben, have visited the Carneal family to express their love and forgiveness. "We've got to remember Michael's family," Ben says. "They're hurting, too."

(Mark Moring, "Split-Second Courage, Ongoing Faith," Christian Reader, January/February 1999.)

Talking At Home:

Read Matthew 6:9–15 and Ephesians 4:32 with your family, and discuss these questions:

• **What do you think of the students' response to Michael and his family?**

• **If you were in a similar situation, how would you respond?**

Ask each family member to describe a time he or she was truly hurting in some way. Did he or she experience God's love and care in that situation, and if so, how or through whom?

Follow the Leader

Mark 8:31-38

3

Jesus Teaches About Commitment

 key question: What's it like to follow Jesus?

 study focus: Teenagers will explore the burdens and benefits that may result from following Jesus.

Key Verse:
"I am not ashamed of the gospel, because it is the power of God for the salvation of everyone who believes: first for the Jew, then for the Gentile" (ROMANS 1:16).

A Look at the Study

Study Sequence	Minutes	What Students Will Do	Classroom Supplies
Getting Started	15 to 20	**Follow Me!**—Explore their choices to follow and discover some consequences of the choices they make.	Poster board, markers
Bible Story Exploration	10 to 15	**J.O.Y.**—Create acronyms describing what it means to follow Jesus.	Bibles, photocopies of "Historical Context" box (p. 31), pens
	20 to 25	**A Life-or-Death Decision**—Re-create the scene between Peter and Jesus and discuss possible reactions of the disciples who followed Jesus.	Bibles, newsprint, markers, tape, paper, pens
Bible Application	15 to 20	**Take Up Your Cross**—Identify their own personal benefits and burdens associated with following Christ.	Bibles, "Take Up Your Cross" handouts (p. 35), pens
	up to 5	**Faith Journal**—Respond in writing to the Key Question.	Index cards, pens
Music Connection	10 to 15	**Runnin'**—Compare following Jesus with running. Use this option at an appropriate time in the study.	CD: "Runnin'" (Track 3), CD player

Age-Level Insight

Junior high students are comfortable following others. Many still feel that there is safety in numbers. Senior high students, however, are anxious to stray away from the closely knit social groups they grew up with and discover new ideas or concepts individually or with new peer groups. As you explore this study with your students, be sure to bring out the idea that Jesus is the perfect person to follow. Whether your students feel comfortable with their peer groups or desire to explore new life experiences with new friends, help them understand that following God first is the best way to live.

As teenagers arrive, greet them warmly, and ask follow-up questions to review last week's study and Key Verse. Ask questions such as "How has Jesus shown that he cares for you?" and "In what ways have the members of your family experienced Jesus' love and care?"

If you used the Faith Journal option last week, take this time to return your students' index cards to them.

Teacher SkillBuilder

Whether your youth group attendance averages four teenagers or forty teenagers, *flexibility* is the key to successful leadership! As you read this study, keep in mind the *greatest* number and the *smallest* number of teenagers you could be working with. Prepare alternative plans for adjusting activities and group sizes to meet your specific needs. For example, for a very small group, make two "Follow Me!" posters, and write two questions on the back of each.

Getting Started

Follow Me!

On each of four sheets of poster board, write the words "Follow me!" Then turn each poster board over and write on the first poster, "Who do you follow?" On the second write, "How do you decide whether to follow?" On the third write, "What can happen when you follow?" On the fourth write, "Why do you follow?"

Have teenagers form four groups, and have each group form a circle. In the center of each circle, place one poster with the words "Follow Me!" facing up.

ASK • **If someone said to you, "Follow me!" how would you respond and why?**

Give groups markers, then have them turn their posters over and read the questions written there. Allow two minutes for group members to write their comments around the questions on their posters. When they've finished, have each group pass its poster to another group. Ask members of each group to read the question on the back of the second poster and add their comments to those written by the first group. Repeat this procedure until each teenager has had an opportunity to comment on all four questions.

Display the finished posters where they can be easily examined. Have students read the written comments and then return to their groups.

ASK • **Did you discover anything interesting about yourself or others through this activity?**

• **What is it like to follow someone?**

• **What if you knew following someone might cause you pain and suffering? What would make you choose to follow anyway? Explain.**

Have volunteers share comments that stood out for them on each poster.

ASK • **What's it like to follow Jesus?**

Bible Story Exploration

J.O.Y.

Give each teenager a Bible, a pen, and a copy of the "Historical Context" box (p. 31). After students have read the Scripture passage and the handout,

SAY **Using the word "joy," the author of the handout created an acronym for what it means to follow Jesus. On the back of your handout, I'd like you create an acronym illustrating what following Jesus means to you.**

Have teenagers share their acronyms.

ASK • **What is it like to follow Jesus?**

• **Have you experienced difficulties or suffering because of your faith? Explain.**

• **What are you willing to endure for your faith in Jesus?**

Historical Context | Mark 8:31-38

This seems to be the first time in the Bible that Jesus openly told his disciples of his coming rejection and death, and they did not like it. Peter, often a spokesman for the group, confronted Jesus about these negative comments—surely things weren't that bad, he thought. The disciples were counting on a great earthly kingdom in which Jesus would lead the Jews in overthrowing the Romans and would place his disciples in important positions. Peter wanted Jesus to change his mind and forget all this talk about dying.

Jesus' rebuke of Peter doesn't suggest that Satan had really taken control of Peter, but that Peter's wrong ideas were ones that Satan might have used to tempt Jesus. Peter's thinking was based on wrong assumptions because he saw things from a purely human point of view. In this case, Peter wasn't acknowledging Jesus as the all-knowing, all-powerful God, but as someone he hoped to influence toward his own desires. Here we see a clear statement about what it means to follow Jesus. Too often we think of God as someone who will give us the things we want, a powerful being who can help us advance our own agendas and achieve our own goals. Instead, truly following Jesus means listening to what he says, discovering his will for our lives, and then obediently following, no matter how attractive or repulsive that may seem to us at the time.

The next segment of the passage takes that concept a step further. A crowd had apparently gathered to hear Jesus, and he wanted to clarify his meaning. This is not a description of what some call "easy believism." Instead, Jesus points out how difficult it may be to become a disciple. Denying oneself means turning away from selfish, self-protective attitudes and seeking the true humility and faith God wants to see in us. In the terms of the "Joy" acronym, it means putting Jesus first, others second, and yourself last.

What does it mean to take up your cross? Jesus no doubt used that wording because he knew he was going to die on a cross. For his disciples to each take up his own cross didn't mean just to endure suffering. It meant to accept the suffering they would face because of their faith in Christ. Sometimes we speak too lightly of "taking up our cross," when in fact we are suffering for our own sins or weaknesses, not for our identification with Jesus. Jesus wanted his disciples to know that their faith might cost them something, a message not too often heard and an event not too often experienced in our culture today. According to church tradition, Peter and many of the other disciples ended up dying for their faith in Jesus.

As he spoke of what it means to follow him, Jesus knew that many in the crowd around him would soon be shouting, "Crucify him!" They would suddenly be ashamed of the one they had followed out of curiosity. These were not followers Jesus would recognize as his own when he returns. Our generation is much like that of Jesus' day. People who claim to be religious—or even Christian—shy away from a bold witness for Jesus. It's easy today to say you believe in God, but it's much more difficult to admit you're a Bible-believing, Jesus-following Christian. Encourage your students to examine their own relationships with Jesus and their witness for him. Help them to see what it means to live a life that is unashamed of Jesus, who did so much for us!

For Extra **Impact**

Before this study, make a three- to five-minute video about following. Include scenes such as a toddler following (or running away from) a parent, dogs running together, or a driver following a car on the freeway. Make these examples as humorous as you like while remaining focused on the Key Question: What's it like to follow Jesus? Use questions similar to these when discussing the video:

• Is following a behavior we have to learn, or is it something we know how to do when we're born? Explain.

• If following is a learned behavior, how do we learn to do it?

• Why do you think some teenagers find it easy to respect and obey people in positions of authority while other teenagers feel it is difficult or even impossible?

A Life-or-Death Decision

Before the study, write these questions on a sheet of newsprint, and post it where everyone can see it.

• What did your character say? What do his words mean to you?

• What do you think your character might have been thinking and feeling during this situation?

Have the group form pairs, and give each person a Bible, paper, and a pen.

SAY I'd like each partner to choose either the character of Jesus or of Peter. Then read Mark 8:31-33 again. As you read, focus on what your character says, does, and might be feeling and thinking. When you've finished, brainstorm answers to the questions listed on the newsprint. Write your answers on the paper I've given you.

Give pairs a few minutes to brainstorm.

SAY Now I'd like you to re-create this scene with your partner. Use the information you just wrote down to help you prepare your scene. You may choose to act out the scene, pantomime the scene, or create a freeze-frame "sculpture" that conveys the emotion of the scene. Try to use modern-day language or ideas as you create your scene.

Give pairs a few minutes to create their scenes, and then have them share their scenes with the rest of the class. After they've all shared, discuss the following questions as a class.

ASK • Why do you think Peter reacted the way he did?

• Why do you think Jesus reacted to Peter the way he did?

• How do you think it might have felt to stand among Jesus' twelve closest friends and witness this scene?

• How do you think *you* would have reacted in this situation?

• What does this passage tell you about what it's like to follow Jesus?

SAY I'd like you to close your eyes and listen while I read the rest of this passage to you. When I've finished, I'll ask some questions. I'd like you to reflect on these questions on your own. Keep your eyes closed.

Read Mark 8:34-38 aloud slowly.

SAY I'd like you to imagine, for a moment, that you're standing in front of Jesus' cross. Imagine that you're reaching out to feel the rough wood. What moments from your life could be symbolized by the feel of the cross? Imagine hearing Jesus' voice, asking you to deny yourself and follow him. How would you feel in that moment? What would it mean to truly deny yourself? Now Jesus asks you to take up your cross. What do you think your personal cross might be? Why does Jesus ask you to do these difficult things? What does it mean to follow Jesus?

Bible Application

Take Up Your Cross

Give each student a "Take Up Your Cross" handout (p. 35), and make sure each person still has a pen and a Bible.

SAY Take a few moments to fill in the segments of the cross for yourself. What benefits and burdens might come from the choice to follow Christ? What does it truly mean to follow Christ?

Give students a few moments to fill in the handout. Then ask volunteers to share some of what they wrote on their crosses. Then invite students to turn to Romans 1:16 and read the Key Verse together.

SAY The Key Verse says, "I am not ashamed of the gospel."

ASK • Are you able to say that with conviction?

• Do you believe it with all of your mind and heart, even if it may mean suffering?

Ask students to personalize the Key Verse by writing it on the middle section of their crosses like this: "I, [student's name], am not ashamed of the gospel."

SAY I'd like you to take your willingness to suffer with Jesus with you this week. Use your cross to remind you of both the benefits and burdens of "taking up your cross," and use the Key Verse to remind you of your commitment to follow Jesus.

Have students form a circle. Close in prayer by having each student in turn say his or her personalized Key Verse.

Faith Journal

Give each student an index card and a pen. Have teenagers write their answers to the following question on their index cards:

• What does following Jesus mean for you?

After teenagers have written their responses, ask them to return the cards to you. Before you meet with the group again, take time to write personal responses to your students on their index cards. You may want to keep a notebook or a box containing copies of these index cards as well as brief notes of prayer concerns and needs your students share using this assessment tool.

For further information about the Faith Journal option, refer to page 5 of the Introduction.

For Extra Impact

As you read the Scripture and the questions for the meditation, you may want to help students get into a more reflective mood by playing soft instrumental music.

For Extra Impact

Give students small wooden crosses to write on instead of the handout.

Tip From the Trenches

To help strengthen the connection between church and home, photocopy the "Taking It Home" page at the end of this study, and either distribute copies to students before they leave or mail them to their homes. Encourage students to complete the reading, activities, and discussion with their families during the coming week.

Ask students to call out the sports they like to play, either competitively or just for fun.

ASK • **How do you prepare to participate in those sports?**

SAY **If we're going to be good at a sport, we have to spend time conditioning and training. Conditioning for many sports includes a great deal of running. I'm going to play a song about running now. Close your eyes and listen. While you listen, think about how you felt the last time you were running.**

Track 3
Play "Runnin' " by Temple Yard.

ASK • **What are some of the things you feel when you're running?**

• **How is this like the way you feel when you're following Jesus?**

SAY **Just as running can make us tired and sore, sometimes following Jesus is difficult. Other times, following Jesus may make us feel exhilarated, just as we feel after a good run. The more we run and condition our bodies, the easier sports and other activities become. In the same way, the more we try to stay close to Jesus, the easier following him and sharing his truth become.**

Runnin'

(recorded by Temple Yard)

We're keeping fit for the fire;
A living faith is our desire.
We give our heart and soul completely;
We'll never stop, we won't grow weary.

We'll just keep running,
Running in the right direction.
We'll just keep running,
Running at a steady pace.
We'll just keep running,
Running under his protection.
We'll just keep running;
We've got no time to waste.

We'll keep a'running,
We'll keep a'running,
Going forward to the other side.
When the punches start a'flying,
We'll have no time for fussing or fighting.
No need to hide or run for cover,
We'll take it in stride, hurrying forward.

We'll fight the good fight, yeah!
We'll run the good race.

On the sidelines,
Oh, so cool,
They're pointing fingers and calling us fools.

Let them mock us one last time
As we're nearing the finish line, yeah.

Look before our eyes; we're gonna win the prize.

Running, running for me life because me smell
*   the trouble coming—*
Running through the night, me never stop until
*   the morning,*
'Til me see the light and me see the day a'dawn-
*   ing.*
You know we are the sheep and the shepherd, 'im
*   a'calling.*
Quit stalling,
Me bawling,
Me sing, say
Running, praying every day to keep the souls that
*   me a'winning.*
Inna the Father's hands the devil no bother try
*   thieving.*
If you walk in the Spirit, then there's no con-
*   demning.*

He Is Worthy

4

Jesus Clears Merchants From the Temple

 key question: How should we worship?

 study focus: Teenagers will explore what it means to reverently worship their Creator.

Key Verse:
"Come, let us bow down in worship, let us kneel before the Lord our Maker" (PSALM 95:6).

A Look at the Study

Study Sequence	Minutes	What Students Will Do	Classroom Supplies
Getting Started	10 to 15	**Awesome Father, Amazing Son**—Discuss ways to worship.	Bible, newsprint, markers, tape
Bible Story Exploration	10 to 15	**The Scene of the "Crime"**—Investigate a "crime scene" and piece together what took place when Jesus cleared the Temple.	Bibles, box, bag of fake money, rope, feathers, newsprint, marker, "Eyewitness Testimonies" handouts (p. 43), paper, pens
	15 to 20	**Anger Management**—Think about current events that call for righteous anger.	Photocopies of "Historical Context" box (p. 40), newsprint, marker, tape
Bible Application	15 to 20	**A.C.T.S. of Reverent Worship**—Create a worship time that reflects their hearts.	Bibles, "A.C.T.S. of Worship" handouts (p. 44), pens, craft supplies, musical instruments, props
	up to 5	**Faith Journal**—Respond in writing to the Key Question.	Index cards, pens
Music Connection	10 to 15	**Heart of the Matter**—Consider those things in the church and in themselves that are not pleasing to God. Use this option at an appropriate time in the study.	CD: "Heart of the Matter" (Track 4), CD player, paper, pens

Age-Level Insight

Young people love to try new forms of worship. They thrive on new forms, new ideas, and experimenting in worship. In their haste to try new things, however, the purpose behind worship might get lost. As you share this study with your students, help them understand the true meaning of worship. Consider having them observe several worship services and write down their questions about worship styles or the purpose behind various elements of worship.

As teenagers arrive, greet them warmly, and ask follow-up questions to review last week's study and Key Verse. Ask questions such as "What does it mean for you to follow Jesus?" and "What kinds of persecution have your family members experienced because of their faith?"

If you used the Faith Journal option last week, take this time to return your students' index cards to them.

For Extra Impact

Select three teenagers to do a choral reading of Psalm 95:1-6. Assign two verses for each student to read. Ask one student to read verses 1 and 4, the second to read verses 2 and 5, and the third to read verses 3 and 6. Instruct these students to space themselves as far apart as possible within the group so their peers will hear each voice and verse distinctly.

Tip From the Trenches

Whenever you read aloud, speak slowly and carefully so your audience can understand each word. Practice several times beforehand to achieve a smooth and expressive reading during the study.

Getting Started

Awesome Father, Amazing Son

SAY **Last week we talked about what it's like to follow Jesus. We learned from one disciple's personal experiences that *believing* in Jesus and *committing to follow* him are two separate issues. Now we're going to dig into a third challenging issue: How should we worship this man who claimed to be the Son of God? Let's start by focusing on God's Word.**

Have teenagers relax, close their eyes, and be still before the Lord. Pause for several seconds until all eyes are closed, and then read Psalm 95:1-6.

SAY **The psalmist invites us to come and worship the Lord, our maker. He suggests we sing for joy, shout out loud, and praise God with music. Is this kind of behavior expected from modern worshippers?**

On newsprint taped to the wall, write the word "worship." Have teenagers form trios.

ASK • **How should we worship?**

Have trios brainstorm as many possible answers to the question as they can. Then ask one person from each trio to write on the newsprint a few of the trio's ideas. Examples of possible answers include singing hymns, lifting hands, singing in a choir, and praying silently.

SAY **There are differing opinions among Christians today on the subject of worship, just as there were differing opinions among worshippers during Jesus' ministry. The Gospel writers tell us about specific times Jesus disagreed with practices that were widely accepted by the people and the culture of first-century Jerusalem. Let's examine one of those incidents.**

Bible Story Exploration

The Scene of the "Crime"

In a location that won't draw too much curious attention from your students, set up a "crime scene" for use during this activity. The scene should include a table and a box to hold items of "evidence" that will help students determine what might have taken place at the scene.

In preparation for this mock investigation, collect or create the following items, and place them in the box:

a bag filled with fake money, a rope, feathers, and a sign that reads "Honest Abraham's Money Exchange."

Your presentation will be most effective if you are careful not to reveal what you plan to do. Just before this activity, set the table on its side, and drape the whip over it. Scatter the pouch, the money, and the feathers (as they might have been scattered in the Bible story); and display the money-changer's sign by leaning it against the table. Practice this arrangement several times in advance to avoid distractions as you set the "crime scene" in front of your audience.

After the scene is set,

SAY This is the scene of a crime. Your job is to investigate and discuss the evidence, determine what happened, and write a statement to release to the media. Now, choose two other people to work with you as an investigative team.

Once students have formed trios,

SAY Each investigator in your trio will have a specific job. The Witness Examiner will closely study the statements of the witnesses to the crime. The Evidence Collector will examine the scene itself to gather evidence, and the Legal Analyst will discuss the crime with the other two investigators and then write the press release. Choose your roles within your trio.

Give each Witness Examiner an "Eyewitness Testimonies" handout (p. 43). Give each Evidence Collector and each Legal Analyst a piece of paper and a pen.

SAY You'll have five minutes to examine the evidence and the eyewitness testimonies. When I call time, you'll have another five minutes to determine exactly what took place and to write a statement that will be presented to the Jerusalem media.

After trios have finished, have the Legal Analysts read their statements to "the press" (the rest of the class).

SAY Now let's read John's account of this story.

Give each student a Bible, and have the Legal Analyst in each trio read John 2:13–22 aloud while the other trio members follow along. Then have trios discuss these questions and share their answers with the entire group after each one.

ASK • Why do you think that what was happening in the Temple made Jesus so angry?

• What does Jesus' reaction tell you about how we should worship?

• What are some inappropriate methods of worship that people sometimes practice today? Why do you think that method is inappropriate?

Anger Management

Give each teenager a copy of the "Historical Context" box (p. 40) to read. When they're finished,

ASK • What do you think of Jesus' reaction to what was going on in the Temple?

For Extra Impact

To make the clues readily connect with the Bible story, consider substituting a cloth pouch for the bag and a whip made out of cords for the rope. Also consider using only white feathers.

Tape a sheet of newsprint to the wall.

ASK • **What are some things going on in our world today that should cause righteous anger?**

Use a marker to write teenagers' answers on the sheet of newsprint. Then discuss each item on the list, asking students how Christians should respond.

ASK • **How can our reaction be a form of worship?**

SAY **We can worship God through our actions and by giving him praise. Let's take some time to give praise to God right now.**

Historical Context | John 2:13-22

Strict regulations guided the activity that was to take place in the Temple. This was to remain a holy place, the dwelling place of God. According to Isaiah 56:7, it was to be a house of prayer.

Unfortunately, the Jewish leaders, who strictly upheld laws that were convenient for them, saw an opportunity for profit in the animals to be sacrificed at the Temple. Any animal to be offered as a sacrifice was to be perfect, free from blemish. And people bringing animals for sacrifice surely chose the best from the flocks and herds. But when Jewish pilgrims brought their animals for sacrifice, the Temple inspectors always found something wrong with them. Then they would conveniently offer animals they had approved—for twenty-five times the going price outside the Temple.

They also were exchanging money—giving people the Temple currency in exchange for their Roman or other foreign coins. The Temple currency was required for paying the Temple tax. From Jesus' disdain of this practice, it is easy to assume that people were also being cheated in this process.

John paints a dramatic picture of Jesus clearing the Temple. With a whip he drove people and animals alike from the Temple courts. The Greek word used here to describe Jesus' action suggests the use of strong force. One might even suggest that Jesus physically threw the merchants out of the Temple. We don't know if only the animals felt the sting of his whip or if the people did too. We do know that Jesus completed his mission and didn't try to escape afterward.

Jesus had seen the conditions in the Temple the night before (Mark 11:11). So it's likely that Jesus' response was not a purely emotional outburst. He saw what was going on in the Temple, he decided overnight what to do about it, and then he took appropriate action. Jesus was angry, and rightly so, but not out of control.

The Jews' response is interesting. They didn't deny that they had been doing wrong. No one asked Jesus why he did what he did. No one angrily struck back at Jesus out of righteous indignation. Their only response was to ask, "How can you prove you have the authority to do this?" When people know they're in the wrong, they often resort to legalistic maneuvering to try to blur the clarity of their guilt. It happened with the Jews then, and it still happens today.

Obviously, the Jews in the Temple had a distorted idea of worship. Psalm 95:6 gives us a brief definition of true worship: bowing humbly before our God. God wants us to acknowledge him and our dependence on him. He wants us to serve him out of genuine gratitude for all he's done for us. And he wants us to love him in the best way we can, even though our love falls so far short of his unconditional love for us.

What does God require of us? "To act justly and to love mercy and to walk humbly with your God" (Micah 6:8).

Bible Application

A.C.T.S. of Reverent Worship

Have students form four groups. Give each student an "A.C.T.S. of Worship" handout (p. 44) and a pen. Make various craft supplies, musical instruments, and props available to your students. For example, you could provide clay or painting supplies, simple instruments such as tambourines and maracas, and supplies for introspection such as paper and pens. Assign each group one of the sections of the handout.

SAY **I'd like you to take the next several minutes to plan a worship time in which you can offer true worship from your heart to the Creator of the universe. Your group will be responsible for the portion of the worship time I've assigned to you. The handout provides a foundation for creating a worship time. Also keep in mind the suggestions for appropriate worship written on the newsprint as well as the unacceptable behavior that Jesus condemned in the Temple courts.**

You may structure your section of the worship time in any way you'd like; just make sure that everyone in your group participates. Remember that you'll be sharing in worship with the whole class. You may use any of the craft supplies or props as you create your part of the worship time.

Allow about ten minutes of planning time, and then bring the groups together. To open the worship time, have teenagers turn to Psalm 95:6 in their Bibles and read the Key Verse together once. Then have students form a circle and kneel. Lead them in saying the Key Verse together three more times, encouraging them to say the verse without using their Bibles. Then ask each group to share its section of the worship time.

To close the worship time, have students kneel in a circle once again. Ask volunteers to offer sentence prayers of praise and thanksgiving to God.

Faith Journal

Give students each an index card and a pen. Have teenagers write their answers to the following question on their index cards:

• **How does God want you to worship him?**

After teenagers have written their responses, ask them to return the cards to you. Before you meet with the group again, take time to write personal responses to your students on their index cards. You may want to keep a notebook or a box containing copies of these index cards as well as brief notes of prayer concerns and needs your students share using this assessment tool.

For further information about the Faith Journal option, refer to page 5 of the Introduction.

for **Younger** *teenagers*

If you feel that younger teenagers might need more direction for this activity, you may want to ask them to use the specific suggestions on the handout. Also encourage them to use their own unique talents and abilities as they're creating their sections of the worship time.

Tip From *the* **Trenches**

To help strengthen the connection between church and home, photocopy the "Taking It Home" page at the end of this study and either distribute copies to students before they leave or mail them to their homes. Encourage students to complete the reading, activities, and discussion with their families during the coming week.

idea:listen

Have kids form groups of four, and give each group a sheet of paper and a pen. Have each group draw a simple outline of a church building.

ASK • Why do you think Jesus was so angry when he entered the Temple area?

SAY I'd like you to imagine that Jesus visited a church in our country today. What do you think he'd find that would make him angry? Inside your church outline, list each item you think of. I'd like you to think of the Christian church across the country rather than focusing on our church or a specific denomination.

Allow each group to present and explain the items in its outline.

SAY I'm going to play a song by Brother's Keeper called "Heart of the Matter." As you listen to the song, think of the things Jesus would find in your heart that would make him angry or sad.

 Track 4
Play the song.

SAY God wants you to change the things in your heart that prevent you from offering sincere worship to him. Fortunately, God comes to us with love and forgiveness rather than a whip. Take a few minutes to ask for forgiveness for the things you listed on your outline and the things you found in your heart.

Play the song again as teenagers pray.

Heart of the Matter
(recorded by Brother's Keeper)

Counterfeit religion has been around awhile—
Mixing in the bad with good, it causes lots of trials.
But just like with diamonds, the fake will be un-
masked.
Lord, help us live our lives for something that will
last.

The heart of the matter is the matter of the heart—
To save a world that's dying, it's the only place to
start.
We can sway one's opinion, turn their point of view,
But only 'til the heart is changed can the old be-
come the new.

Wherever you may go, wherever you may be,
God is always watching; he sees the Pharisees.
I pray that he does surgery on my life and yours—
Transplant his heart of love, replace this evil core.

We can analyze, second-guess,
We can argue who loves Jesus best.
But the only heart you can look into
Is the one inside of you.
But go ahead and feel around
From your head to your feet.
But when the song of God is sung,
You'll recognize the beat.

Eyewitness Testimonies

Name: Solomon

Identification: Jewish male, thirty-seven years old

Occupation: Merchant; sells young bulls for the purpose of Temple sacrifice

Comments: "Just look at this mess! My bulls are running through the streets of Jerusalem, and it's all *his* fault—that crazy Nazarene who says he's the Son of God! Who could believe such a man?"

Name: David

Identification: Jewish male, forty-eight years old

Occupation: Merchant; sells sheep for Temple sacrifice

Comments: "My poor lambs! They are scared to their very death! How can I guarantee them to be unblemished after such emotional trauma? I will take him to court for what he's done—that rabbi, Jesus!

Name: Simon

Identification: Jewish male, seventy-seven years old

Occupation: Merchant; sells doves for Temple sacrifice

Comments: "The man was raving, I tell you! He was cracking that whip and yelling, 'How dare you turn my Father's house into a market!' To *me*, Simon the dove seller, he said these horrible things! What right did he have to destroy my business? And what did he mean when he said 'my Father's house,' anyway?"

Name: Abraham

Identification: Jewish male, fifty-three years old

Occupation: Money-changer; sells bills and coins acceptable to the priests

Comments: "Arrest him! Crucify him! He overturned my table, and my money is scattered everywhere! I saw children scrambling for the coins as they rolled into the street! I've heard stories about this Jesus, and I swear to you—by all that's holy—he is a lunatic!"

research required

[t h i n k]

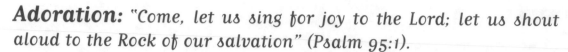

A.C.T.S. of Worship

[think]

Adoration: *"Come, let us sing for joy to the Lord; let us shout aloud to the Rock of our salvation"* (Psalm 95:1).

- **Worship suggestion:** Think of a way to show the Lord how much you love him and why you wish to honor him! You might consider creating a "love collage" depicting ways people show their love to God or leading the group in a brainstorm session in which we think of all the different reasons we love and honor God.

Confession: *"Come, let us bow down in worship, let us kneel before the Lord our Maker"* (Psalm 95:6).

- **Worship suggestion:** Include a brief time for personal confession before the Lord, trusting him to wash away sin with his righteousness. You might consider writing a prayer litany, leading the group in a time of reflection, or giving the group some questions or thoughts to write about.

Thanksgiving: *"Let us come before him with thanksgiving and extol him with music and song"* (Psalm 95:2).

- **Worship suggestion:** Ask yourself, "How can I express my praise to God and my thankfulness for his blessings?" You might consider writing an act of praise, leading the group in a praise song, or creating a "praise skit."

Submission: *"In his hand are the depths of the earth, and the mountain peaks belong to him. The sea is his, for he made it, and his hands formed the dry land"* (Psalm 95:4-5).

- **Worship suggestion:** How should we humble ourselves in worship and ask for the Lord's guidance and protection? You might consider creating a sculpture (either human or clay) depicting ways we can humble ourselves in worship or sharing personal stories about how the Lord has guided and protected each person in your group in the past.

Driving Home the Point:

God Available

Almighty God

who made the

delicate field daisy and

the limitless reaches of space...

thank You for being

God Available.

No, more even than available.

Thank You for seeking me

First—for searching along

the agonizing road to

Golgotha,

then finding me blindly supplying

nails for Your Son's hands.

And when

I finally found

You, Lord,

Your bleeding hand was

reaching for mine.

(Susan L. Lenzkes, **When the Handwriting on the Wall Is in Brown Crayon**)

Talking At **Home:**

Read Psalm 139:1-14 with your family, and discuss these questions:

• **What do you think God loves most about you?**

• **What do you love most about God?**

• **How can you show God that you love him?**

• **Why does God want you to show that you love him?**

Ask each family member to share a time he or she felt very close to God. How did he or she respond? How did each experience demonstrate reverent worship?

Permission to photocopy this handout from FaithWeaver™ Youth Bible Studies granted for local church use. Copyright © Group Publishing, Inc., P.O. Box 481, Loveland, CO 80539. www.faithweaver.com

God So Loved the World

John 3:12-21

5

 key question: Why did God send Jesus?

 study focus: Teenagers will explore the meaning of God's most precious gift—his Son.

Key Verse:
"For God so loved the world that he gave his one and only Son, that whoever believes in him shall not perish but have eternal life" (JOHN 3:16).

A Look at the Study

Study Sequence	Minutes	What Students Will Do	Classroom Supplies
Getting Started	10 to 15	**Market Niche**—Identify needs that products meet and discuss the needs Jesus meets.	Old magazines and newspapers
Bible Story Exploration	10 to 15	**By Rote**—Discuss the significance of John 3:16.	Bibles, photocopies of "Historical Context" box (p. 49)
	25 to 30	**Dimensions of Need**—Create a triptych illustrating three needs that God sent Jesus to meet.	Bibles, "3-D" handouts (p. 54), pens, large roll of paper, markers, scissors, construction paper, glue sticks, yardstick, pencils, tape
Bible Application	10 to 15	**My Need**—Identify their own personal need for Jesus as Savior and offer a prayer of confession to him.	Construction paper, scissors, pens, legal pad, tape
	up to 5	**Faith Journal**—Explore the Key Question and respond in writing.	Index cards, pens
Music Connection	10 to 15	**Only One**—Creatively explore the difference Christ has made in their lives. Use this option at an appropriate time in the study.	CD: "Only One" (Track 5), CD player, newsprint, marker, tape

Age-Level Insight

Teenagers are mature enough to understand that John 3:16 is more than a verse they can recite in their sleep or a sign they see at football games. They are ready to decide if they will go beyond understanding Christ's words and start living them. Challenge your teenagers to move past the childish understanding of John 3:16 as a nice and important verse to a verse that requires them to make a decision about how they are going to live their lives.

As teenagers arrive, greet them warmly, and ask follow-up questions to review last week's study and Key Verse. Ask questions such as "How does God want us to worship him?" and "What experiences of reverent worship did your family members share?"

If you used the Faith Journal option last week, take this time to return your students' index cards to them.

Getting Started

Market Niche

Ask students to think of and name some of the most successful products from the past few years. Ask students why they think those products were so successful. Point out that most successful products meet needs—either real needs or desires that consumers have come to believe are needs ("I have to have that logo on my shoes, or I'll never make the team").

Have students form pairs. Give each pair one or more magazines or newspapers. Ask each pair to find at least one ad and determine the need the product is trying to meet. Assure students that there is no one right answer. For example, an ad may be stating that a certain brand of toothpaste meets the need for a fresh-feeling mouth while, on another level, trying to convince people that the product will also meet their need for romance.

Give pairs a few minutes to find their ads, and then have each pair share its ad and name a need the product might meet.

ASK • **What's your response when someone tries to sell you—either in person or through an ad—a product you don't need?**

• **When we talk about Christianity, some people just don't "buy" it. Why do you think that is?**

Point out that many people don't believe they need Jesus.

ASK • **Why did God send Jesus? What needs was Jesus sent to meet?**

Bible Story Exploration

By Rote

Hold a contest to see who can say John 3:16 the fastest. Then have your students compete to recite other things they have memorized such as the Pledge of Allegiance, The Lord's Prayer, "Amazing Grace," and the Apostles' Creed. Then give each student a Bible and a copy of the "Historical Context" box (p. 49).

SAY **You've all probably heard John 3:16 at one time in your life, and many of you can probably recite it from memory. Our familiarity with this important passage can cause us to miss its meaning. I'd like you to read John 3:12-21 and the handout I've given you. Then find a partner to talk about what John 3:16 means to your life.**

Give teenagers an opportunity to share what they've discussed with the entire group.

ASK • **Why did God send Jesus?**

• **What significance does Jesus have in your life?**

Historical Context | John 3:12-21

In this passage, Jesus is talking with Nicodemus, a Pharisee and a member of the Sanhedrin, the Jewish religious ruling council. Nicodemus had come to Jesus under the cover of darkness to find out for himself who Jesus really was. Nicodemus believed that Jesus was from God (John 3:2), but he didn't want people to think he was one of Jesus' followers.

Jesus launched into the conversation by making it clear that new birth is the only way to God's kingdom. For Nicodemus, a strict follower of the Law who thought obedience to a set of rules was his ticket to heaven, the concept of a "new birth" was tough to grasp. He had trouble accepting that all his good works and intentions wouldn't get him into God's kingdom. So in this passage, Jesus clearly states what it takes to get to heaven—and why God sent him to earth.

Jesus' reference to Moses' lifting up the snake in the desert refers to a time God sent poisonous snakes among the Israelites to punish them for rebelling against him. Those who had been bitten were dying. But God in his mercy instructed Moses to make a snake of bronze and lift it up on a pole where all could see it, promising safety to all who looked upon it. All who believed God and looked at the snake were spared from death. In the same way, Jesus would be lifted up on the cross, and as people looked to him in faith, they would be spared from eternal death for their sins.

Why did God do it? Why did he send his own Son to die an agonizing death on the cross? The answer is clear in verse 16: "For God so loved the world that he gave his one and only Son, that whoever believes in him shall not perish but have eternal life." In this sentence Jesus summarizes God's entire plan of salvation. The Greek word used for "love" in this verse is agape, the highest type and form of loving described in the Bible. When one stops to contemplate the magnitude of God's sacrifice, it seems nearly incomprehensible. A normal human father might give up his life to save his own child's life. A mother might even give up her life to save another mother's child. But for a parent to give the life of his or her child for the sake of others who don't even care seems out of the question. And then to think of God, the creator, sustainer, and owner of the universe giving up his *only* Son for sinful, rebellious people—that seems truly unimaginable. But God did it. For me. For you. For them. What amazing love!

Perhaps Nicodemus was thinking that Jesus' presence in the world condemned it. Jesus seemed to be pointing out that the religious leaders were doing everything wrong. No doubt Nicodemus felt condemned by things Jesus had said. But in verse 17, Jesus makes it clear that the condemning part of his presence was only to help people to an awareness of their sin. The real purpose for Jesus' coming was to save those who saw their need for him and who responded to him in faith.

Jesus' message for Nicodemus and for us today is that following all the religious rules won't win us God's favor. God has a different plan, because all the good we can ever do won't wipe out a single sin. Only Jesus' sacrifice on the cross, paying the death penalty for us, makes it possible for us to enter heaven. And only our response in faith to that offer and to the Holy Spirit's working in our lives will seal the deal.

We don't know how Nicodemus responded to Jesus that night. But we do know that he stood up for Jesus' right to speak for himself before the Sanhedrin (John 7:50-51). We also know that he brought a large quantity of expensive embalming materials for Jesus' burial after the crucifixion. But that's the last we hear of Nicodemus in the Bible.

For a truly dramatic visual representation of the passage, have students create a "stained-glass window." Have them cut paper from the roll to fit a window in your meeting space or in some other area of the church. Instruct groups to draw a fairly simple illustration on the paper and then cut out the major portions (the face, the hand, the snake, and so on) and replace them with colored tissue paper. When the finished project is hung in a window, the light will come through the tissue paper and give the effect of stained glass.

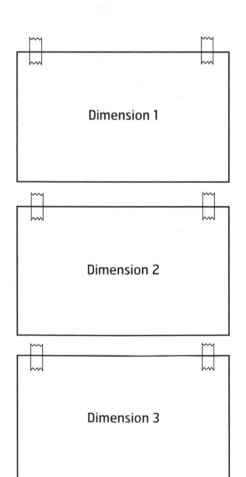

Dimensions of Need

Form three groups. Give each group Bibles, pens, and "3-D" handouts (p. 54). Set out the following art supplies: a large roll of paper at least three feet wide (the kind used to cover tables works well), markers, scissors, construction paper, glue sticks, a yardstick, and pencils. Add any other supplies you think your students might enjoy using.

Assign each group one of the "dimensions" listed on the handout.

SAY **We're going to create a floor-to-ceiling triptych—a three-part piece of art. Each group will create one part of the triptych to represent one of the three dimensions of the passage we're studying. You'll use paper from this roll as the "canvas" for your section, and you may draw with markers, cut out shapes from the construction paper, or do anything else you decide in your group to do. Because the three sections of a triptych go together, they should all be the same size, so be sure to cut a seven-foot** [or whatever height works for your room] **length of paper for your canvas. And create your art so that the three pieces will hang next to each other from ceiling to floor.**

Instruct the members of each group to read the relevant passage listed on the handout, discuss the questions, and then work together to illustrate their passage for their section of the triptych. When everyone has finished, have the groups tape their pieces of art to the wall so that the three dimensions are next to each other (see illustration in margin).

Ask someone from the first group (Dimension 1) to read aloud John 3:12-15 and Numbers 21:8-9. Ask the questions in the "Dimension 1" section of the handout. Invite students from all of the groups to comment on elements of the triptych section that illustrates the passage.

Next ask someone from the second group (Dimension 2) to read aloud John 3:17-19. Ask the questions in the "Dimension 2" section of the handout.

Finally, invite someone from the third group (Dimension 3) to read aloud John 3:19-21. Ask the questions in the "Dimension 3" section of the handout.

Point out that the group has now heard all of John 3:12-21 except for one very important verse. See if anyone knows which verse was left out. If they need help, tell them it's the Key Verse written on the handout: John 3:16.

With the students, read the verse in unison, and then

ASK • **According to this verse, why did God send Jesus?**

• **Has this activity affected your understanding of why God sent Jesus?**

To help students begin to memorize John 3:16, have them write the verse as a title for their triptych: Roll out a long length of the paper, and have each student write the verse somewhere on the paper. Post the title banner above or next to the triptych.

Bible Application

My Need

Set out construction paper, scissors, a legal pad, and pens. Have students rejoin their original groups, then give the following assignments:

- **Dimension 1 group, cut out construction paper snakes, and label each snake with a fatal sin that people today are dying from. Don't focus just on actions that might result in physical death; instead, remember that all sin ultimately leads to eternal death unless we look to Jesus.**

- **Dimension 2 group, on separate sheets of legal paper, write specific charges that people today might face if they were called into God's court.**

- **Dimension 3 group, list some of the specific "evil deeds" done by people who love the darkness. Write the deeds in a way that will allow you to incorporate them into your triptych section in a few minutes.**

After a few minutes, have students read what they've written and tape each paper onto the appropriate triptych section. (For example, students will add the "sin" snakes to Dimension 1.)

When all the groups have responded, remind students that all the things they've listed are reasons God sent Jesus.

Close this session by asking students to sit quietly in front of the artwork.

SAY **Silently choose the dimension of the triptych that speaks to you. Now imagine yourself in that picture. Ask yourself, "Why did God send Jesus for *me*?" What is the sin that has its teeth in you as badly as any poisonous snake? What charge could be read against you in a heavenly court of law? What thoughts or actions would you cringe to have revealed in the light? Why do you need Jesus?**

After a few moments of silence, invite students who have not decided to live their lives for Jesus to do so.

SAY **If you believe in Jesus, you shall not perish but have eternal life. If you've put your trust in Jesus you are no longer lost in sin but are free and alive. Enjoy and live that truth.**

End your time with a prayer thanking God for sending Jesus to meet our overwhelming need for a Savior.

Tip From the Trenches

If the original groups consisted of more than six students per group, form smaller groups to help ensure that everyone participates in the discussion.

for Younger teenagers

Younger students who are proud of the artwork they created earlier may be upset about "defacing" it by taping anything to it. Allow them simply to read what they've written and post their pages near the triptych.

Faith Journal

Give each student an index card and a pen. Have teenagers write their answers to the following question on their index cards:

- **Why do *you* need Jesus?**

After teenagers have written their responses, ask them to return the cards to you. Before you meet with the group again, take time to write personal responses to your students on their index cards. You may want to keep a notebook or a box containing copies of these index cards as well as brief notes of prayer concerns and needs your students share using this assessment tool.

For further information about the Faith Journal option, refer to page 5 of the Introduction.

Music Connection

idea:listen

[music]

Write the following idea starters on a piece of newsprint, and post the newsprint where students can see it.

• How God's gift has changed my life
• A time I only "loved God when I was strong"
• How I think God wants me to respond to his gift

Direct students' attention to the newsprint.

SAY **I'd like you to think about what you would say in response to these idea starters while I play "Only One" by Jill Phillips for you.**

 Track 5
Play the song.

Have students form trios and share their ideas about each idea starter. Then allow volunteers to share their insights with the whole group.

ASK • **What difference does believing in Jesus make for you during hard times?**

• **What difference does believing in Jesus make for you in good times?**

• **What would your life be like without Jesus?**

SAY **When you put your complete faith and trust in Jesus, he changes everything about your life. He gives you strength for the hard times and greater joy in the good. No matter how you are feeling today, you can put your trust in Christ and constantly walk with him. Take a minute to pray, telling God that you put more trust in him and want him to take all of your life—the good and the bad.**

Only One

(recorded by Jill Phillips)

You are the only road that leads me home,
But I only take you when I'm lost.
You are the only one who loves me in my weaknesses,
But I only love you when I'm strong.

You are the only water giving life,
But I only drink you when I thirst.
Now that I've taken all these things for granted all this time,
You'd think I'd get what I deserve.

But you cared so much for me
That you gave your only Son,
And you'd do it all again
If I was the only one.

I know I don't deserve your love for me,
And I know it's something I can't earn.

You are the only one whose love does not depend upon
What I can give you in return.

You alone created every star in every galaxy;
You also made these lines upon my hands.
How could someone so great have such a deep concern for only me?
I don't think I'll ever understand.

You...oh, you—
You'd do it all again
If I was the only one.

John 3:12-21 describes three dimensions of the salvation Jesus brought to the world. Work through your assigned "dimension" below.

Dimension 1

Read John 3:12-15 and Numbers 21:8-9.

• In what way is Jesus like the snake that Moses lifted up in the desert?

• How was Jesus "lifted up"?

• According to these verses in John, why did God send Jesus?

• How could you visually depict what Jesus said in these verses?

Dimension 2

Read John 3:17-19 together, and discuss the following questions:

• If salvation were decided in a courtroom, who do you think would be in the following roles?

　• judge

　• prosecuting attorney

　• defense attorney

　• defendant

• What would the verdict be?

• According to these verses, why did God send Jesus?

• How could you visually depict what Jesus said in these verses?

Dimension 3

Read John 3:19-21 together, and discuss the following questions:

• What does it mean that "light has come into the world" (verse 19)?

• What are some of the benefits of light?

• How is living as a Christian like living in the light?

• According to these verses, why did God send Jesus?

• How could you visually depict what Jesus said in these verses?

KEY VERSE

"For God so loved the world that he gave his one and only Son, that whoever believes in him shall not perish but have eternal life" (JOHN 3:16).

Permission to photocopy this handout from FaithWeaver™ Youth Bible Studies granted for local church use. Copyright © Group Publishing, Inc., P.O. Box 481, Loveland, CO 80539. www.faithweaver.com

[think]

Taking It Home

Driving Home the Point:

A life ring is no good to a person who refuses to admit he's drowning.

Talking At Home:

Read Romans 3:21-26 with your family, and discuss these questions:

• **Why is it so difficult for people to acknowledge that they are sinners?**

• **What most amazes you about God's response to sinful people?**

Ask family members each to describe a time they realized they were in big trouble and what they did to get help. Ask family members to compare their feelings in those crises and after being rescued with their feelings about sin and how Jesus rescues them.

[take home]

Giving With Gusto

Mark 12:41-44

6

Jesus Notices a Widow's Giving

 key question: What can you give to God?

 study focus: Teenagers will explore specific, concrete ways to give cheerfully to God.

Key Verse:
"Each man should give what he has decided in his heart to give, not reluctantly or under compulsion, for God loves a cheerful giver" (2 CORINTHIANS 9:7).

A Look at the Study

Study Sequence	Minutes	What Students Will Do	Classroom Supplies
Getting Started	10 to 15	**The Joy of Giving**—Share memories about giving and receiving.	
Bible Story Exploration	10 to 15	**Give It Up**—Discuss times of generosity and stinginess.	Bibles, photocopies of "Historical Context" box (p. 59)
	10 to 15	**Method Acting**—Dramatize the attitudes revealed by the characters in the Bible passage.	Bibles
Bible Application	20 to 25	**Giving With Gusto**—Identify ways to give time and money.	"Giving With Gusto" handouts (p. 63), pens
	5 to 10	**Put Your Money Where Your Mouth Is**—Make specific giving commitments and personalize the Key Verse.	Bibles, fake money, pens
	up to 5	**Faith Journal**—Respond in writing to the Key Question.	Index cards, pens
Music Connection	10 to 15	**Everything**—Explore what it means to give everything to God. Use this option at an appropriate time in the study.	CD: "Everything" (Track 6), CD player, envelopes, paper, pens, offering plate

Age-Level Insight

Material possessions mark the difference between popularity and unpopularity for many junior and senior high students. While some teenagers might not admit it, many struggle with a desire to have the "right" possessions in order to gain the "right" friends. So giving to God feels difficult for them. In reality, giving to God probably won't adversely affect your teenagers' economic status. However, the changes that take place in teenagers once they develop giving attitudes and hearts may cause them to be ostracized by some peers. As you explore this study with your students, help them grasp the benefits of giving to God. And help them see that those benefits outweigh the costs.

As teenagers arrive, greet them warmly, and ask follow-up questions to review last week's study and Key Verse. Ask questions such as "Why did God send Jesus?" and "How have your family members experienced being 'rescued' from sin?"

If you used the Faith Journal option last week, take this time to return your students' index cards to them.

For Extra Impact

Challenge students each to give one other person in the group something right now. Give only these instructions and see what happens.

Teacher SkillBuilder

Help teenagers become comfortable with sharing personal spiritual insights by moving them through a series of progressively more revealing questions. This process works best when you start by asking an unintimidating question that can be answered with a purely factual statement, then ask a related question that goes a little deeper emotionally, and finally ask a question that deals with a personal spiritual matter.

Getting Started

The Joy of Giving

Have students form groups of four to share their responses to the following questions. Have each group member respond to the first question before moving on to the next question.

ASK
- **Where were you living when you were eight years old?**
- **What was one of your favorite Christmas or birthday presents when you were eight or close to that age?**
- **What is one of your earliest memories of giving a present to someone else?**
- **When did you discover the joy of giving?**
- **What can you give to God?**

Bible Story Exploration

Give It Up

Have teenagers form pairs to discuss the following statements and questions.

- **Describe a time you were stingy.**

ASK
- **How did you feel afterward?**
- **Why did you act the way you did?**
- **Describe a time you were generous.**
- **How did you feel afterward?**
- **Why did you act the way you did?**

Give volunteers an opportunity to share some of their discussions with the entire group. Give each student a Bible and a copy of the "Historical Context" box (p. 59), and have teenagers read Mark 12:41-44 and their handout.

ASK
- **Why do you think Jesus was pleased with the widow's giving?**
- **What can you give God?**
- **How can you tell if God is pleased with your giving?**

Method Acting

Have students stay in their groups of four.

SAY **In your group, read Mark 12:41-44 again. Discuss the attitudes you think the rich people might have had and the attitude you think the widow had. Then choose three people to act the part of the rich people. Have each "rich person"**

Historical Context | Mark 12:41-44

At the beginning of this passage, Jesus does a peculiar thing: He sits down to watch people making their offerings. What was he thinking? These were freewill offerings, not the Temple tax required by Jewish law. Why did Jesus want to see what people were giving? We don't know all the reasons, but one was apparently to teach his disciples a lesson. Jesus had talked about money earlier, explaining the need to pay taxes and to give to God. Now he was ready to teach a visual lesson.

While Jesus—and presumably some of his disciples—sat watching, numerous rich people gave large amounts of money. The disciples, who were from the lower economic classes, were probably amazed at some of the fortunes offered by these wealthy Jews. They may not have even noticed the poor widow who dropped her two coins into the treasury box. These were the smallest coins in the Roman Empire. It took forty of these to make up a day's wages. In terms of today's wages, they would have been worth no more than a couple of dollars each. Yet Jesus knew how big the widow's gift was.

As a symbol of their marriage, Jewish women in Jesus' day wore headpieces on which coins were sewn. Wealthy women displayed a number of large coins; poorer women displayed smaller coins. This woman may have given the last two coins from that headpiece to God. Wherever the coins came from, she gave all she had.

Some Christians today might consider the widow's giving foolish—she didn't have to give both coins; she didn't have to give even one coin. After all, she needed that money just to stay alive. But that kind of thinking is precisely what Jesus was teaching against. If we give only part of what we have—of what we are—to Jesus, we're holding back. Jesus wants all of us. He wants us to give him all we have and all we are and to trust him for the results.

Which of the givers in this passage are you more like? Who are your class members more like? As you explore this passage, challenge people to examine what they're giving to God. Are they giving just a small portion of their time, money, talents, and commitment to God? Is God getting the leftovers after they've taken care of all their wants? Or are people giving as the poor widow gave, risking all they have on God? The widow's choice is not an easy one, but it is one that honors God.

demonstrate, without speaking, a different attitude. For example, one rich person might bring his offering with dramatic flourishes to make sure that everyone notices his generosity. Another might be stingy and have a hard time letting go of her offering. The third rich person might give with a joyful expression—not all rich people are bad! Have the fourth person in your group act the part of the widow. In a few minutes I will read the story while you act it out.

Give students a few minutes to read the passage again and discuss their roles. Then read the passage aloud as all the rich people act their parts at the same time and all the widows act their parts at the same time.

ASK • **What attitude were you trying to convey in your role?**

• **How do you think Jesus would have responded to that attitude?**

• **Which character in this story do you identify with? Why?**

Tip From the Trenches

If you have only two foursomes, you can read the passage twice, having one foursome perform while the other watches. With three or more groups, however, such repetition becomes monotonous, and it is better to have all the groups act at once.

What will you say when a student asks whether we, like the widow, ought to give everything we have to God? Younger students will do best with the concrete instruction in the Bible Application section: Make a commitment to give, and then cheerfully meet that commitment. But older teenagers can also explore the more abstract ideas expressed in Colossians 3:17, which directs believers to do *everything* for God. Help students grapple with what it means to give one's schoolwork, one's relationships, and one's vocational choices to God. Assure students that they don't have to have the final answer to these complex issues and that they will continue to grow in their understanding as they continue to mature in their faith.

Tip From
the Trenches

Have students read all of 2 Corinthians 9 to learn the context of the Key Verse, which makes it clear that Paul is demonstrating a motivation for cheerful giving, not an excuse for not giving.

• **Why did Jesus say that the widow gave more than the others?**

• **What can we learn from the widow's actions and attitudes?**

Have students follow along in their Bibles as a volunteer reads the Key Verse, 2 Corinthians 9:7.

ASK • **What can we learn about attitude from this verse?**

• **What does it mean to give "under compulsion"? What examples can you give of this?**

• **Do you think this verse means you shouldn't give if you don't feel like it? Explain.**

• **How do you become a cheerful giver?**

• **What can you give cheerfully to God?**

Bible Application

Giving With Gusto

Explain that in this activity, you'll focus on two areas of giving: money and time. Hand out pens and the "Giving With Gusto" handout (p. 63).

Have students form pairs.

ASK • **In what ways can you give financially to God?**

Have pairs write their ideas in the "money" sections of the handout. For example, in the box titled "How You Can Get Some to Give," students could list existing sources of income (such as an allowance or income from a baby-sitting job) as well as other ideas they haven't tried yet (such as mowing lawns or working out an arrangement with parents to take a sack lunch several times a week in order to give away the money they would have spent on a hot lunch). In the "Ways to Give It" box, they could list causes they would like to support. After a few minutes, bring all the students back together to report their ideas to the rest of the group. Encourage teenagers to add to their lists any good suggestions they hear from others.

As students mention ideas,

ASK • **What would it look like to be a cheerful giver in this situation?**

• **What would it look like to give reluctantly or under compulsion?**

• **What difference would it make if you gave gladly or reluctantly?**

• **In what ways can you give your time to God?**

Have pairs write their ideas in the "time" sections of the handout. For example, in the "How You Can Get Some to Give" box, students could list ways to free up time for service (such as getting up early on Saturday or cutting back on long phone conversations). In the "Ways to Give It" box, they could list ministries or service projects with which they could serve as well as less-structured ways to give their time (such as helping a classmate with homework or spending a lunch hour with someone needing a friend). After a few minutes, bring all the students together to report their ideas to the rest of the group. Encourage students to add to their lists any good suggestions they hear from others.

As students mention ideas,

ASK • **What would it look like to be a cheerful giver in this situation?**

• **What would it look like to give reluctantly or under compulsion?**

• **What difference would it make if you gave gladly or reluctantly?**

Put Your Money Where Your Mouth Is

Challenge students to make a specific commitment to give to God this week. Hand out fake money, and have students write this version of the Key Verse on the blank side:

"I will give what I have decided in my heart to give: [specific gift of time and/or money]—not reluctantly or under compulsion, for God loves for me to be a cheerful giver."

Encourage students to keep the fake money in their wallets to remind them of their commitments.

Faith Journal

Give each student an index card and a pen. Have teenagers write their answers to the following question on their index cards:

• **What can you give cheerfully to God?** ❓

After teenagers have written their responses, ask them to return the cards to you. Before you meet with the group again, take time to write personal responses to your students on their index cards. You may want to keep a notebook or a box containing copies of these index cards as well as brief notes of prayer concerns and needs your students share using this assessment tool.

For further information about the Faith Journal option, refer to page 5 of the Introduction.

For further information about the Faith Journal option, refer to page 5 of the Introduction.

---

for Younger teenagers

Younger teenagers often don't have a lot of discretionary spending money. You can motivate them to financial stewardship by helping them find a cause they can get excited about and then helping them think of creative ways to earn money. Consider brainstorming ideas for a fundraiser for a Christian cause and then carrying it out as a group.

Tip From the Trenches

To most effectively equip your students to live out the application of this study, provide them with a list of opportunities for meaningful ministry within your church and community. Help them choose ministries that match their abilities and interests, and then help them get involved.

Tip From the Trenches

To help strengthen the connection between church and home, photocopy the "Taking It Home" page at the end of this study, and either distribute copies to students before they leave or mail them to their homes.

idea:listen

Give each student an envelope, a sheet of paper, and a pen or pencil.

ASK • **What do you think God wants you to give to him?**

SAY As I play the song "Everything" by Watermark, I'd like you to listen for the song's ideas about what God wants us to give him.

 Track 6
Play "Everything" by Watermark.

ASK • **What do you think it means to give everything to God?**

• **Are there some things in your life that are more difficult to surrender to God? Explain.**

SAY Now I'd like each of you to use your sheet of paper to write an offering prayer to God. In your prayer, tell God that you give him everything. Name the things that are more difficult for you to give. When you're finished, fold up your prayer and put it in the envelope.

I'll pass an offering plate around. I'd like you to place your envelope in the plate as a sign of your offering to God.

While you pass the plate, play "Everything" again.

Everything

(recorded by Watermark)

Everything—Lord, I bring everything.
I lift my hands and show you what I bring.
I bring you everything.

Everything—Lord, I bring everything.
Your heart rejoices, and the angels sing
When I bring everything.

All of my heart I give.
My life is to you an open door.
And Spirit, you're welcome to walk right through
And take with you...

Everything—Lord, I bring everything.
All I want is for you to be,
To be my everything.

From the album *Watermark*. Words and music by Nathan and Christy Nockels. Copyright © 1995 Rocketown Music/Sweater Weather Music (ASCAP). All rights reserved. Used by permission.

Giving With Gusto

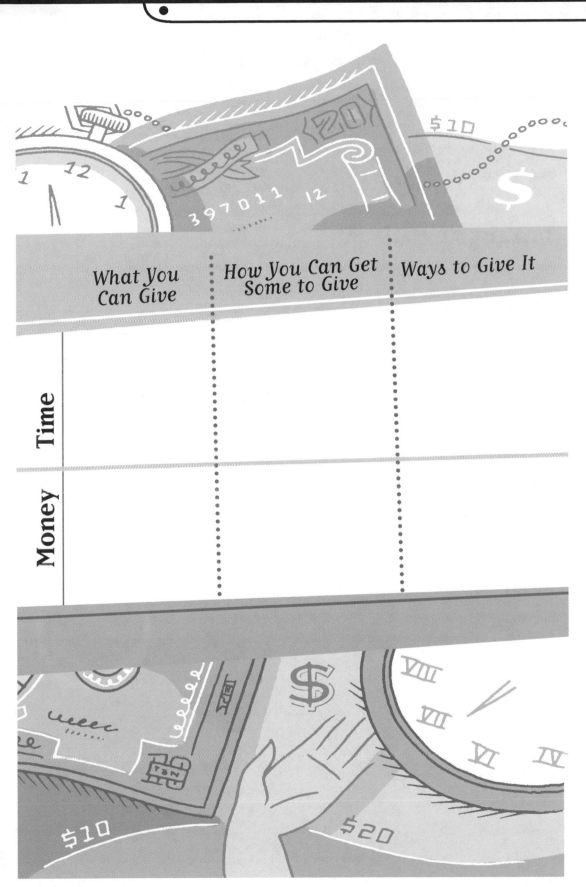

	What You Can Give	How You Can Get Some to Give	Ways to Give It
Time			
Money			

[think]

research
required

OK
to copy

Permission to photocopy this handout from FAITHWEAVER™ YOUTH BIBLE STUDIES granted for local church use. Copyright © Group Publishing, Inc., P.O. Box 481, Loveland, CO 80539. www.faithweaver.com

Driving Home the Point:

"You must give time to your fellow men—even if it's a little thing, do something for others—something for which you get no pay but the privilege of doing it."

(Albert Schweitzer)

Talking At Home:

Read 1 Timothy 6:17-19 with your family, and complete this survey:

• **In what ways is our family rich? Check all that apply.**

___ money

___ love

___ good times together

___ great meals

___ humor

___ a specific skill: _____

___ other: _____

___ other: _____

• **How could we share our wealth with someone else?**

___ Give $_____ to _____.

___ Share love with _____ by _____.

___ Invite _____ to join our good times on _____ [date].

___ Invite _____ for dinner or bring a meal to _____.

___ Cheer up _____ by _____.

___ Use our skill (_____) to help _____.

___ Other: _____

___ Other: _____

• **Which of these are we willing to do?**

• **When will we do them?**

Honoring Jesus

Mark 11:1-11

7

People Rejoice as Jesus Enters Jerusalem

 key question: How can we honor Jesus?

 study focus: Teenagers will explore ways to respond to Jesus.

Key Verse:
"That at the name of Jesus every knee should bow, in heaven and on earth and under the earth, and every tongue confess that Jesus Christ is Lord, to the glory of God the Father" (PHILIPPIANS 2:10-11).

A Look at the Study

Study Sequence	Minutes	What Students Will Do	Classroom Supplies
Getting Started	5 to 10	**Respecters of Persons**—Act out different identities.	
Bible Story Exploration	10 to 15	**Dear Diary**—Create journal entries from the perspectives of witnesses of Jesus' triumphal entry.	Bibles, paper, pens, photocopies of "Historical Context" box (p. 67)
Bible Application	20 to 25	**Roll Play**—Discover biblical titles for Jesus and play a game to raise questions about how to respond appropriately to Jesus.	Bibles, pens, "Roll Play" handouts (p. 71), scissors, tape
	up to 5	**He Is Lord!**—Praise Jesus by singing a song derived from the Key Verse.	Bibles
	up to 5	**Faith Journal**—Respond in writing to the Key Question.	Index cards, pens
Music Connection	10 to 15	**Own Me**—Individually create a symbol of themselves and honor Jesus by laying it before him. Use this option at an appropriate time in the study.	CD: "Own Me" (Track 7), CD player, craft supplies, cross or Bible

Age-Level Insight

Adolescents are emotionally charged. Try to help your teenagers go beyond the "mountaintop" experiences they may have during your meetings, missions, or conferences and carry their worshipful attitudes into their day-to-day lives. As you explore this study with them, help students understand that God is present with them every day and in every situation they face. If they understand this, they'll have an easier time honoring Jesus in *everything* they do.

Last Week's Impact

As teenagers arrive, greet them warmly, and ask follow-up questions to review last week's study and Key Verse. Ask questions such as "What have you given cheerfully to God in the past week?" and "How did your family members choose to give to others?"

If you used the Faith Journal option last week, take this time to return your students' index cards to them.

Getting Started

Respecters of Persons

Have your students form pairs. Explain that one person in each pair will leave the room. While those volunteers are absent, their partners will be told the absent members' new identity. When the absent members return, they will have to figure out their own new identity based on the way their partners are acting toward them.

Have one member from each pair leave the room, and then tell the remaining partners that they are to act as if they are the loyal subjects of their absent partners, who are each Queen Elizabeth.

Readmit the absent partners to the room, and have those who remained try to demonstrate their identity by the way they act. Have the partners who left the room try to guess their own identity as well as that of those who remained.

Play additional rounds using the following identity sets:

• The absent partner is a two-year-old child; the remaining partner is the parent.

• The absent partner is a baseball player; the remaining partner is the coach.

After a few rounds,

ASK • How could you tell who you were supposed to be?

• How did your identity affect the way your partner acted toward you?

Point out that a person's identity often determines how others act toward that person. For example, an action that is perfectly respectful with a close friend might be inappropriate with a teacher or a governor.

ASK • What are some basic actions that show respect?

• How can we honor and show respect to Jesus?

Bible Story Exploration

Dear Diary

Give each teenager a sheet of paper and a pen.

SAY I'd like you to imagine that you were one of the people, other than the disciples, who were celebrating Jesus' triumphal entry as described in Mark 11:1-11. Read Mark 11:1-11, then create a journal entry describing what you felt and saw as you cheered Jesus.

After students have completed this journal entry, distribute a copy of the "Historical Context" box (p. 67) to each student.

SAY Now read the handout I've given you, and write another journal entry describing your feelings when you saw Jesus on the cross only five days after his triumphal entry.

Allow students to share their entries.

ASK • Why did the people who celebrated Jesus' entry into Jerusalem give him honor and praise?

• What about Jesus did the people accurately understand?

• What were their misconceptions about Jesus?

• Why do you give Jesus honor and praise?

• How do you honor Jesus?

Historical Context | Mark 11:1-11

The beginning of this passage always strikes a new reader as unlikely. Who would have allowed the disciples to take a young donkey—something poor people didn't possess—simply because they said the Lord needed it and would return it? We don't know if this was a completely supernatural event or if these people knew the disciples and Jesus, but whatever the case, it happened. God had prepared for this moment in history.

And this moment in Jewish history had long been anticipated. Zechariah 9:9 predicts that the Messiah would come "gentle and riding on a donkey, on a colt, the foal of a donkey." Without question, the Jews along Jesus' path made this connection and knew what it meant. Their celebration made this clear as they covered Jesus' path with their outer robes and palm branches—a demonstration of honor and submission.

By riding a donkey, Jesus not only fulfilled Zechariah 9:9, he also indicated that he came in peace. In Jewish culture a donkey was no less valued or respected than a horse, but to enter Jerusalem on a horse would have indicated warlike intentions. Riding a donkey, Jesus represented a king who came to bring peace.

The cries of the people were also significant. As they shouted "hosanna," they were saying, "Lord, save us!" As they referred to Jesus as "he who comes in the name of the Lord" and spoke plainly of "the coming kingdom of our father David," they were making clear references to the Messiah predicted many times in the Old Testament.

After the excitement of his triumphal entry, Jesus and his disciples left Jerusalem to spend the night in Bethany, where Mary, Martha, and Lazarus lived. No mention is made of the crowd following them. After all the cheering had died down, everyone must have gone home. What do you suppose the disciples were feeling and thinking during that hourlong walk to Bethany? Jesus had spoken earlier of his imminent death, but the day's events probably encouraged them to think about Jesus being made king. How could things possibly turn against him as Jesus said they would? As events unfolded, the disciples' heads must have been spinning. Throngs honored Jesus that day, but only a few days later the disciples hid in fear of the authorities, trying to find a way to live for the crucified Jesus.

Fortunately, we know the rest of the story. After the Resurrection, everything changed. And that's how it should be in our lives. When we choose to live for Jesus, everything changes. We don't honor him just by cheering and praying and singing great worship songs. We honor him—as the disciples did—in every facet of our lives. We honor him through our worship but also through our obedience, service, witness, and gratitude.

Bible Application

Roll Play

Form pairs. Distribute pens and the "Roll Play" handout (p. 71). Make sure everyone still has a Bible. Provide scissors and tape.

Assign half the pairs to work on the section of the handout titled "Who Is Jesus?" Instruct them to look up the passages listed on the handout and write a brief title for Jesus or description of Jesus based on each passage in each of the six faces of the flattened cube on the handout.

When pairs have filled in all the sides of their cubes, have them cut out and assemble the cubes. If students need help determining Jesus' identity in each of the passages, here are the answers:

- Matthew 16:16—Christ, Son of God
- John 6:35—bread of life
- John 8:12—light of the world
- John 10:11—good shepherd
- John 14:6—the way, the truth, and the life
- Philippians 2:11—Lord

Assign the other pairs to work on the section of the handout titled "How Can We Honor Jesus?" Instruct them to think of everyday situations in which it might be challenging to honor Jesus.

Have pairs write one scenario or situation in each of the six faces of the flattened cube on the handout. Encourage pairs to describe specific situations. For example, urge them to make a general situation such as "at school" more specific by describing a specific event at school. Here's an example: "You're not allowed off campus, but a lot of people leave at lunch time anyway. Some people you've been eager to become friends with ask you to go off campus for lunch with them." When they have filled in all the sides of their cubes, have them cut out and assemble the cubes.

Now have each pair with a "Who Is Jesus?" cube join with a pair with a "How Can We Honor Jesus?" cube.

SAY **Roll the "How Can We Honor Jesus?" cube, and read the situation on the top. Then roll the "Who Is Jesus?" cube, and read the title or description of Jesus on the top. In your foursome, discuss how that aspect of Jesus' identity helps you know how to honor him in that situation. For example, suppose the situation is "You're not allowed off campus, but a lot of people leave at lunch time anyway. Some people you've been eager to become friends with ask you to go off campus for lunch with them." If the title that comes up is "good shepherd," you might realize that Jesus wants you to obey the rules that have been set up by the school and at the same time he cares about you and your relationships. So** you can be confident that you can build those relationships in a way that doesn't break school policy.

As foursomes work together, circulate to make sure that students are able to make connections between the situations and who Jesus is.

ASK • **What is an appropriate response to someone who is Lord? the Good Shepherd?**

• **How does this description of Jesus encourage you in this situation?**

• **How does it warn you?**

After a few minutes, bring the entire group together and

ASK • **What were some of your most challenging situations?**

• **How can we honor Jesus in those situations?**

• **What difference will it make in your life this week to acknowledge who Jesus is and respond appropriately?**

He Is Lord!

Have students follow along in their Bibles while a volunteer reads aloud the Key Verse, Philippians 2:10-11. Remind students that a wonderful way to honor Jesus is to sing his praises. Sing the praise song based on the Key Verse, "He Is Lord:"

> He is Lord; he is Lord;
> He is risen from the dead, and he is Lord!
> Every knee shall bow, every tongue confess
> That Jesus Christ is Lord!

Faith Journal

Give each student an index card and a pen. Have teenagers write their answers to the following question on their index cards:

• **How will you show honor and respect to Jesus?**

After teenagers have written their responses, ask them to return the cards to you. Before you meet with the group again, take time to write personal responses to your students on their index cards. You may want to keep a notebook or a box containing copies of these index cards as well as brief notes of prayer concerns and needs your students share using this assessment tool.

For further information about the Faith Journal option, refer to page 5 of the Introduction.

for Younger teenagers

Keep active kids involved by turning your "roll play" into role-plays: Instead of having foursomes discuss responses to the situations, have them act out what they might do to honor Jesus in those situations.

Tip From the Trenches

If you don't know this song, lead your students in chanting the Key Verse instead.

Tip From the Trenches

To help strengthen the connection between church and home, photocopy the "Taking It Home" page at the end of this study, and either distribute the copies to students before they leave or mail them to their homes. Encourage students to complete the reading, activities, and discussion with their families during the coming week.

idea:listen

Set out simple craft supplies, such as construction paper, markers, scissors, and tape. Ask teenagers to use the supplies to create a symbol of themselves. For example, a student may make a paper soccer ball or a musical note to symbolize who he or she is. Set a cross or Bible at the front of the room.

SAY **I'm going to play a song called "Own Me" by Ginny Owens. As you listen, identify how the singer chooses to honor Jesus.**

 Track 7
Play the song. Then have teenagers form pairs to discuss the following questions.

ASK • **What did this song have to say about honoring Jesus?**

• **How have you honored Jesus with your life?**

• **What changes are you going to make in your life to bring honor to Jesus?**

SAY **I'm going to play the song again. Close your eyes as it plays and think about one way you can honor Jesus. As a sign of your commitment to honor Jesus, lay the symbol of yourself you created at the foot of this cross** [or on this Bible]. **Kneel there and make your commitment to God in silent prayer.**

Play the song as many times as necessary to give each student a chance to make a commitment.

Own Me

(recorded by Ginny Owens)

Got a stack of books so I could learn how to live;
Many are left half-read, covered by the cobwebs
*   on my shelf.*
And I got a list of laws growing longer every day;
If I keep pluggin' away, maybe one day I'll perfect
*   myself.*
Oh, but all of my labor seems to be in vain,
And all of my laws just cause me more pain;
So I fall before you in all of my shame,
Ready and willing to be changed.

Own me,
Take all that I am,
And heal me!
With the blood of your Lamb,
Mold me with your gracious hand,
Break me 'til I'm only yours.
Own me!

You call me daughter,
And you take my blame;
And you run out to meet me
As I cry out your name.
So I fall before you in all of my shame.
Lord, I am willing to be changed.

Who Is Jesus?

Together, read each passage. Based on the passages, write brief titles or descriptions of Jesus, using one of the squares below for each passage. Then cut on the solid lines, fold on the dotted lines, and tape the cube together.

• Matthew 16:16 • John 6:35 • John 8:12 • John 10:11 • John 14:6 • Philippians 2:11

How Can We Honor Jesus?

Together, think of six situations in which it might be challenging to honor Jesus. Write one situation in each of the squares below. Then cut on the solid lines, fold on the dotted lines, and tape the cube together.

[t h i n k]

research required

Talking About It

Driving Home the Point:

"To know whom you worship, let me see you in your shop, let me hear you in your trade, let me know how you rent your houses, how you get your money, how you kept it and how you spent it."

(Theodore Parker, **Sermon of Conventional and Natural Sacraments**)

Talking At Home:

Read Proverbs 14:31 with your family, and discuss these questions:

• **How can we worship and honor God by what we do?**

• **What are some ways, other than singing praises, that you have honored God?**

• **Why do you think Jesus is worthy of honoring?**

This week, encourage each family member to take a few minutes each morning to plan at least one way to honor God. At the end of the week, discuss whether family members noticed a difference in the way they felt and acted.

everywhere

[take home]

Hoping for Easter

Mark 16:1-8

Jesus Rises From the Dead

key question: Why do we celebrate Easter?

study focus: Teenagers will explore why Easter is so crucial to their faith and their lives.

Key Verse:
"Jesus said to her, 'I am the resurrection and the life. He who believes in me will live, even though he dies' " (JOHN 11:25).

A Look at the Study

Study Sequence	Minutes	What Students Will Do	Classroom Supplies
Getting Started	10 to 15	**The Truth About Easter**—Discuss various objects and emotions associated with Easter.	"The Truth About Easter" handouts (p. 79)
Bible Story Exploration	10 to 15	**Easter Background**—Share insights about the Easter story.	Bibles, photocopies of "Historical Context" box (p. 75), pens
	20 to 25	**I Was There**—Explore the story of the Crucifixion and the Resurrection from the "points of view" of some of the objects involved.	Bibles, index cards, small paper bag, pens, paper
Bible Application	15 to 20	**A Hunt for Hope**—Share their hopes and participate in a hunt for hope.	Slips of paper, pens, plastic Easter eggs, permanent markers, Easter candy
	up to 5	**Faith Journal**—Respond in writing to the question "What does Easter mean to you personally?"	Index cards, pens
Music Connection	10 to 15	**Magdalene**—Consider the Resurrection from the perspective of Mary Magdalene. Use this option at an appropriate time in the study.	CD: "Magdalene" (Track 8), CD player, paper, pens

Age-Level Insight

Many teenagers have had so much exposure to the Easter story that the Easter celebration has become somewhat stale and mechanical for them. If you notice this happening with your teenagers, encourage them to think beyond the obvious truths of the Resurrection. Probe their understanding by using "why" questions. Begin by asking them why Jesus' resurrection is important. If a student answers, "Because it shows Jesus' victory over death," ask him or her why that is significant. Continue this type of questioning until you see an opportunity to ask a teenager what difference Easter has made or can make in his or her own life. This type of probing and personalizing will help your teenagers see that Easter has simple and profound truths for their everyday lives.

Getting Started

The Truth About Easter

SAY To begin, I'd like you to think of all of the things that come to mind when you think of Easter. Just call them out as you think of them.

Give students several seconds to call out all of their Easter associations.

SAY Now I'd like you to think of all of the emotions that may be associated somehow with Easter. Call them out as you think of them.

Again, give students several seconds to call out emotions.

SAY Two significant emotions expressed in the Easter story are fear and hope.

ASK • How do you think fear might be a part of Easter? How about hope?

• Why do we celebrate Easter?

Give each student a "Truth About Easter" handout (p. 79).

SAY I'd like you to take a moment to read what one author has to say about the true meaning of Easter. When you've finished, please find a partner.

Give students a few minutes to read the handout and then find partners.

SAY Now discuss these questions with your partner.

ASK • What does this quotation say to you?

• According to this author, why do we celebrate Easter?

Ask pairs to share ideas with the entire group.

Bible Story Exploration

Easter Background

Give each student a Bible, and ask everyone to read Mark 16:1-8. Then give everyone a copy of the "Historical Context" box (p. 75) and a pen.

SAY Please read the handout I've just given you. As you read, I'd like you to underline any statements that are particularly meaningful or interesting to you.

When teenagers have finished, have them form pairs and share their insights. Then allow volunteers to share their insights with the whole group.

Historical Context | Mark 16:1-8

One of the saddest statements in the whole Bible is Mark 14:50. Jesus had poured himself into the twelve disciples for three years. But when he surrendered to the authorities, "everyone deserted him and fled." Jesus, the Son of God, was left to face an agonizing and undeserved death alone.

Fortunately, the story doesn't end there. Easter changed everything!

The first question skeptics ask about Jesus' resurrection is "Why do the Gospel writers all tell different stories?" To answer that question, think about an exciting event in your life at which several people were present. If you asked them to tell about the events of that day, would all their versions of the story be exactly the same? Of course not. We all see things from different perspectives and remember different details of what we see. That's exactly what happened with the Gospel writers' telling of Jesus' resurrection. All seeming contradictions arise out of their slightly different views of events and can easily be resolved when one accepts that truth. In fact, if all the accounts were exactly the same, a critic would say that the authors had collaborated to make up the story. And, thanks to these different viewpoints, the accounts we have—as orchestrated by God—give us a more nearly complete picture of what happened than if only one Gospel had been written.

The angel's proclamation "He has risen!" was the most wonderful news anyone could have given to Jesus' followers. He was alive, and they were to meet him! Why did the angel mention Peter specifically? Peter—the bold one—had fearfully denied Jesus three times the night of his trial and then had broken down and wept (Mark 14:66-72). Now that Jesus was alive, Peter would likely wonder if Jesus would accept him. The angel left no doubt of Jesus' forgiveness by telling the women at the tomb, "Go tell his disciples and Peter."

Why do we celebrate Easter? The Apostle Paul eloquently tells us, "If Christ has not been raised, your faith is futile; you are still in your sins. The sting of death is sin, and the power of sin is the law. But thanks be to God! He gives us the victory through our Lord Jesus Christ" (1 Corinthians 15:17, 56-57). What more could we ask? "Thanks be to God for his indescribable gift!" (2 Corinthians 9:15).

ASK • **What about the Easter story is amazing to you?**

• **Why do we celebrate Easter?**

I Was There

Before the study, write the following objects and Scripture references on index cards, and place them in a small paper bag.

• a purple robe and a crown of thorns (Mark 15:16-20)

• the beam of a cross (Mark 15:21-23)

• Jesus' clothes (Mark 15:24-32)

• a sponge (Mark 15:33-41)

• some linen cloth and a large stone (Mark 15:42-47)

• a large stone (Mark 16:1-8)

Have pairs combine to form groups of four. Give each group paper and pens.

SAY Since we know that Easter is more than a nice spring celebration, let's learn more about the difference it really does make in our lives. To do that, we'll be reading and exploring the story of the Crucifixion and the Resurrection.

There are several cards in this bag. On each card is written one or two of the objects found in the story of the Crucifixion and the Resurrection, along with a Scripture reference telling where in the Bible the object is mentioned. In a moment, one member of your group will draw a card out of the bag. I'd like you to read the Scripture reference together, taking note of the object as you read. Then I'd like you to take a few minutes in your group to recall your portion of the story by writing a first-person monologue from the point of view of the object or objects. For example, if your object is a crown of thorns, you might start your monologue by saying something like this: "I am the crown of thorns the soldiers put on Jesus' head. It was a horrible scene I witnessed that day..." You may want to refer to the Scripture verses that precede yours to make sure you understand the context of the events you will be describing.

Give students about ten minutes to read their Scriptures and write their monologues. Then have one volunteer from each group read aloud the group's assigned Scripture and another volunteer share the monologue.

After the story has been told,

ASK • What's your reaction to hearing the story told in this way?

• What do you think it would have been like to really witness these events?

• After completing this activity, what new insights do you have into the question "Why do we celebrate Easter?"

Have foursomes read the Key Verse, John 11:25. Ask them to whisper the verse to one another in their groups, one at a time, and then whisper the verse in unison.

ASK • What are some of the ways that our world "whispers" the news of the Resurrection?

• What are some other ways that we could celebrate the news of the Resurrection?

Bible Application

A Hunt for Hope

Have students return to the pairs they formed in the "Truth About Easter" activity.

SAY The story of Easter changes everything in our lives. When Jesus conquered death, he also conquered all of the fears that cripple us. We celebrate Easter because it reminds us of that fact. We celebrate Easter to help us remember that we can live our lives with hope. We need to stop whispering the good news. We need to shout our hope to the world!

I'd like you to take a few moments to share your hopes with your partner. Tell about something you're hoping for in your life. For example, you might share that you're hoping to have a closer relationship with God or that you're hoping to make a difference with your life. Don't be afraid to share— telling about hope is the first step to living it.

After students have finished sharing, hand each student a plastic egg, a pen, and a slip of paper. Give each pair a permanent marker. Have some Easter candy available, but don't give it to the students yet.

SAY Now that you've heard each other's hopes, I'd like you to share hope with your partner. I'd like you to write a "note of hope" for him or her. Write a few sentences of hope and encouragement to that person based on the hope he or she shared, reminding him or her of our reasons to hope. Please include the Key Verse in your note. Don't let your partner see what you're writing. Be sure to sign your note, then fold it and place it in a plastic egg. Then write the person's name on the egg with the permanent marker. When you've finished, come and put some Easter candy in the egg, and give the egg to me.

When students have finished, ask two volunteers to take the eggs outside (if the weather permits) and hide them. If the weather doesn't allow you to go outside, have students close their eyes while the hiders conceal the eggs around the room.

SAY Because we're human, we have a hard time letting go of fear and living in the power of the Resurrection: hope. Hope is the reason we celebrate Easter. God has taken away all reason for fear. This changes everything. Easter is so much more than just a fun celebration; we can now spend each day living in the hope we've found.

Let students search for their "hope" eggs. Encourage them to take their eggs home and put them in a visible place to remind them of the hope they have because of Easter.

Faith Journal

Give each student an index card and a pen. Have teenagers write their answers to the following question on their index cards:

• What does Easter mean to you personally?

After teenagers have written their responses, ask them to return the cards to you. Before you meet with the group again, take time to write personal responses to your students on their index cards. You may want to keep a notebook or a box containing copies of these index cards as well as brief notes of prayer concerns and needs your students share using this assessment tool.

For further information about the Faith Journal option, refer to page 5 of the Introduction.

idea:listen

Have students form pairs, and give each pair a sheet of paper and a pen or pencil.

SAY We're going to listen to a song examining the Resurrection from a unique point of view—that of Mary Magdalene. As you listen, imagine what the experience must have been like for Mary Magdalene.

Track 8
Play "Magdalene" by Chris Rodriguez.

ASK
- How do you think Mary Magdalene felt when she discovered the empty tomb?
- How do you think you would have responded in this situation?

SAY In your pair, I'd like you to write a fictitious letter to Mary Magdalene, telling her the truth of the Easter story. Share with her how the story has affected your lives, and help her to understand that the event is a cause for celebration, not grief.

Have pairs share their letters with the group.

SAY Like Mary Magdalene in this story, many people don't understand what the Resurrection is all about. Let's tell others about what happened and what it means to us.

Magdalene

(recorded by Chris Rodriguez)

She is cloaked in morning's darkness—
Magdalene—
Now running to the tomb,
Her heart is so consumed.
The stone is rolled away.
"Wherein lies my master,
The one who brought to me such life?"

Can you tell me why you're weeping,
Magdalene?
Have they taken him away?
Is he not in the grave?
Tell me who you're seeking,
Magdalene—
The one that they have crucified?

Woman, where's your faith now?
Start believing.
Remember what he said;
He'd come back from the dead.
He'd never leave you or forsake you.
Do you believe that he's the Lord?

Why would you seek, as you do,
The living among the dead?
He is not here; now do not fear.
Believe what he has said.

Do you seek the man of sorrows,
Magdalene?
Then look into my eyes and see that he's alive—
The spotless Lamb of God now and forever,
The holy one of Israel.

Say to them
That I am
Risen and alive,
Victorious the Lord and Christ,
God's begotten Son.

Can you tell me why you're weeping,
Magdalene?
Have they taken him away?
Is he not in the grave?
I am the one you're seeking,
Magdalene.
I'm the Resurrection and the life.

From the album *Beggar's Paradise*. Words and music by Chris Rodriguez and Glenn Garrett. Copyright © 1999 Still Working for the Man Music/Rodge Podge Music/BMI/Cut Above Music/ASCAP. All rights reserved. Used by permission.

Do you know what the most frequent command in the Bible turns out to be? 'Be good'? 'Be holy'? 'Don't sin'? No. The most frequent command in the Bible is *'Don't be afraid.'*

The irony of this surprising command is that, though it's what we all really want to hear, we have as much difficulty, if not more, in obeying this command as any other.

This surprising command bursts in upon a world in which we eat, sleep, and breathe fear.

The resurrection of Jesus issues the surprising command: don't be afraid; because the God who made the world is the God who raised Jesus from the dead, and calls you now to follow him. Believing in this God means believing that it is going to be all right; and this belief is, ultimately, incompatible with fear.

(N.T. Wright, *Following Jesus*)

[t h i n k]

research required

everywhere

[take home]

Driving Home the Point:

Easter is much more than a celebration of spring; it reminds us that in raising Christ from death, God has created a world in which we have nothing to be afraid of. It's very hard to live without all of our fears and worries, but Easter keeps reminding us that God has made everything all right. We can live with hope. We don't often talk about our fears or our hopes within our families. But it's important "stuff" to talk about.

Talking At Home:

Read Psalm 118:14-24 together. Then use the following sentence starters to share some of your fears and Easter hopes with each other.

• An event in the past that was frightening for our family was…

• I am afraid of…

• A situation in our family in which we could use God's help is…

• A time I did not have much hope was…

• Something that I really don't need to worry about is…

• Signs of hope that I see in our family life are…

• As a family, I think we're doing better with…

• I hope God is working to…

Faith and Doubt

John 20:19-31

Jesus Appears to His Disciples

 key question: What does it mean to have faith?

 study focus: Teenagers will discover that they can know God with certainty even though they cannot see him.

Key Verse:
"Now faith is being sure of what we hope for and certain of what we do not see" (HEBREWS 11:1).

A Look at the Study

Study Sequence	Minutes	What Students Will Do	Classroom Supplies
Getting Started	5 to 10	**Face-to-Face Faith**—Place themselves on a continuum to demonstrate whether their faith would be stronger it they could see Jesus face-to-face.	Masking tape
Bible Story Exploration	10 to 15	**They Had It Easy**—Decide whether it was easier for people to have faith in Jesus while he was on earth.	Bibles, photocopies of "Historical Context" box (p. 83), pens
	20 to 25	**Seeing Is Believing**—Reflect on the Bible passage from Thomas' point of view.	Bibles, "Seeing Is Believing" handouts (p. 87), pens
Bible Application	20 to 25	**Hands-On Faith**—Share truths that will help them hold on to faith.	Bibles, pens, construction paper, scissors, "Seeing Is Believing" handouts (p. 87), nails
	up to 5	**Faith Journal**—Respond in writing to the Key Question.	Index cards, pens
Music Connection	10 to 15	**Concerns**—Explore specific concerns and doubts they have about God and thank him for his grace when they doubt. Use this option at an appropriate time in the study.	CD: "Concerns" (Track 9), CD player, index cards, pens

Age-Level Insight

Teenagers are just beginning to understand concepts like faith. Younger ones try to grasp the meaning of faith, while older students try to understand how they can practice faith in their daily lives. As you explore this study with your students, help younger ones come to a deeper understanding of faith. Help older students understand how they can trust God in every situation they face.

As teenagers arrive, greet them warmly, and ask follow-up questions to review last week's study and Key Verse. Ask questions such as "What does Easter mean to you personally?" and "What are some of your family's hopes and fears?"

If you used the Faith Journal option last week, take this time to return your students' index cards to them.

for **OLDER** *teenagers*

Give older teenagers a more developed profile of Thomas as a devoted seeker by exploring these passages with them:
• John 11:7-16, which shows Thomas' willingness to die for Jesus;
• John 14:5, in which Thomas' question shows his eagerness to learn from and follow Jesus; and
• John 21:1-14, in which we see Thomas working alongside the other disciples—and this time not missing out on Jesus' appearance!

Getting Started

Face-to-Face Faith

Using masking tape, mark a line down the center of the floor. Designate one end of the line as "strongly agree" and the other end as "strongly disagree."

SAY Place yourself somewhere on this line depending on how strongly you agree or disagree with this statement: "My faith would be much stronger if I had lived when Jesus lived."

Ask volunteers from various points on the continuum to explain why they chose to stand where they did. Try to form groups of people from different parts of the continuum to provide a variety of perspectives on the topic. Then form groups of four to discuss the following questions.

ASK • How might talking with Jesus face-to-face, hearing his teaching, or seeing his miracles strengthen your belief in him?

• How might not being able to see Jesus face-to-face force you to rely more on faith?

• What does it mean to have faith?

Bible Story Exploration

They Had It Easy

Give each student a Bible, a copy of the "Historical Context" box (p. 83), and a pen. Ask everyone to read John 20:19-31 followed by the handout.

SAY The handout asserts that it may be easier for us to believe in Jesus today than it was for those who actually saw him. On the back of your handout, state whether you agree or disagree with this assertion, then list the reasons that support your position.

Give students a minute to create their lists, then ask volunteers to share.

ASK • What does it mean to have faith?

• Is it difficult for you to have faith? Explain.

Seeing Is Believing

Have students remain in their groups of four. Give each group Bibles, pens, and the "Seeing Is Believing" handout (p. 87). Instruct groups to work through the handout, reading the passages and sharing their responses to each question before moving on to the next question. Make sure everyone in each group responds to each question.

When the groups have finished, call them back together.

ASK • What do you think Thomas learned about himself from this experience?

Historical Context | John 20:19-31

Hiding in a room with the doors locked "for fear of the Jews." That's where Jesus found his disciples the evening of his resurrection day! It's easy to be hard on them and wonder, "What were they *thinking*? Shouldn't they have been celebrating?" However, we should walk in their sandals before criticizing them. They knew Jesus had been crucified. Some, no doubt, had seen him die. They had seen the display in the heavens and on earth when God's Son gave up his spirit (Matthew 27:45, 51-54). They had heard from the women that Jesus had risen, but they hadn't seen him. Had the women been hallucinating because they *wanted* to see Jesus? How could it possibly be true? Confusion must have ruled their thoughts and conversation that evening. What makes us think we'd have responded any differently?

Jesus must have looked somewhat different in his new spiritual body. Mary didn't recognize him at first outside the tomb (John 20:14). And apparently Jesus' appearance to the disciples didn't immediately allay their fears because his first words were "Peace be with you!" Then he showed the disciples the wounds in his hands and side to certify his identity. It may have taken a moment, but finally the disciples' fears and confusion fell away, and they were overjoyed!

Having faith was not easy for these first-century disciples. Thomas was really no different from the others. He's just pointed out as a doubter because he said he wouldn't believe the resurrection until he had seen Jesus and touched him. The other disciples demonstrated by their actions that they doubted Jesus' resurrection until they actually saw him.

It's easy to think that those living in Jesus' day had an advantage over us in developing faith. But that's not necessarily true. In actuality, we may have the advantage. Jesus' life, death, and resurrection didn't fit the disciples' expectations of the Messiah. When he died then rose from the dead, they had to reconsider all their preconceived notions of the Messiah. They had to match Jesus' actions with what the Old Testament Scriptures predicted about the Messiah. Only then could they fully have faith.

Our advantage is that the results of their struggles are recorded for us in the Bible. We have Thomas' declaration: "My Lord and my God!" We have the book of Acts that tells us of the disciples' bold faith and proclamation of the good news about Jesus. And we have the epistles that explain details of faith and what it means. If one accepts that the Bible comes from God, all the evidence one could possibly need for faith is there.

What does it mean to have faith? Read Paul's words in Philippians 3:7-9: "But whatever was to my profit I now consider loss for the sake of Christ. What is more, I consider everything a loss compared to the surpassing greatness of knowing Christ Jesus my Lord, for whose sake I have lost all things. I consider them rubbish, that I may gain Christ and be found in him, not having a righteousness of my own that comes from the law, but that which is through faith in Christ—the righteousness that comes from God and is by faith."

Faith means trusting Christ for everything. It means believing in his sacrifice on the cross for us and living a life of gratitude for what he's done. It means giving up any hope of winning God's favor by our human efforts. It means seeking Jesus above all else.

- **What do you think he learned about Jesus?**

- **In what ways do you think it might be more "blessed" to be a believer who has not seen Jesus in the flesh?**

Ask groups to share their written responses to this question: What does it mean to have faith?

Bible Application

Hands-On Faith

ASK
- Do you ever feel as if "believing without seeing" means you shouldn't have questions about your faith? Explain.

- What evidence do we have that God wants us to ask questions and seek answers to them?

Point students to such passages as Matthew 7:7-8 (God wants us to ask, seek, and knock; and he will respond) and John 20:31 (the Bible is written specifically so that we can know things that will lead us to faith).

SAY Even though we can't see Jesus face-to-face, our belief is not blind. Our faith is built on truths that we can confidently know. Think for a few moments about something you know about God that would help strengthen someone else's faith. It might be a specific verse that tells you about God's character, a quality of God, or an action God has taken.

Hand out construction paper, pens, and scissors. Have each person trace his or her hand on a piece of paper, cut out the hand shape, and write his or her name on the palm. Have students sit in a circle and pass the paper hands around the circle, writing one truth about God on a finger of each hand that comes by.

When each hand has ten truths written on it (one on each finger on each side), have students find their own paper hands and silently read what is written.

ASK
- What truth do you find most encouraging for your faith?

- What statement do you have a question about?

- How do the truths written on your paper hand add to your understanding of what it means to have faith?

Ask students to close their eyes and reflect silently on these questions:

ASK
- What questions or struggles make it hard for you to have faith?

- When do you especially need to hold on to the truths you know about Jesus?

- What would it take in that situation for you to say to Jesus, "My Lord and my God"?

Have students open their eyes. Ask each person to use the back of the "Seeing Is Believing" handout to rewrite the Key Verse as a prayer for faith in the difficult situation he or she has just been recalling.

Urge students to silently pray their written prayers. Give teenagers each a nail as a tangible reminder to make Thomas' confession of faith their own.

For Extra Impact

Read aloud Isaiah 44:1-5, emphasizing verse 5: "One will say, 'I belong to the Lord'; another will call himself by the name of Jacob; still another will write on his hand, 'The Lord's,' and will take the name Israel." Invite students to write "The Lord's" under their names on their paper hands.

for Younger teenagers

Give younger teenagers this model for writing their own prayers:
"Lord, help me to have faith, to be sure of this hope:

_____
_____
and certain of
_____
_____ ,
even though I cannot see it."

Faith Journal

Give each student an index card and a pen. Have teenagers write their answers to the following question on their index cards:

• **What does it mean for you to have faith?**

After teenagers have written their responses, ask them to return the cards to you. Before you meet with the group again, take time to write personal responses to your students on their index cards. You may want to keep a notebook or a box containing copies of these index cards as well as brief notes of prayer concerns and needs your students share using this assessment tool.

For further information about the Faith Journal option, refer to page 5 of the Introduction.

Teacher SkillBuilder

When several small groups are engaged in a project or an extended discussion, they probably won't all finish at the same time. Be prepared with one or more of the following suggestions to keep students focused on the subject while they wait for other groups to finish:

• **Ask additional questions.** Have a few related questions in mind, or ask the group to list as many contemporary parallels to the truth of the passage as they can. In this study, for example, you could ask students to list examples of believing something without seeing it for themselves.

• **Have students illustrate the event or the truth of the passage.** Keep a supply of paper and markers on hand for students to use. Students illustrating the events of this study, for example, might opt to draw a frame-by-frame, comic-strip version of the events or create a montage of faces expressing the various emotions people might have felt.

• **Ask students to find songs that deal with the issues addressed.** Provide songbooks for students to look through, and encourage them to think of other contemporary songs that relate to the passage. For this study, students might find songs relating to doubt, faith, or the events of Christ's post-resurrection appearances.

Give each student an index card and a pen or pencil.

SAY As you listen to this song, called "Concerns," by Clear, I'd like you to jot down some of your personal concerns that sometimes make believing in Christ difficult.

 Track 9
Play the song.

ASK • What are some of the concerns you listed?

• How can you respond to such concerns?

Take the time to talk about each concern as necessary. Don't be afraid to say, "I don't know," if you're not sure how to answer a question. But make certain to investigate the question and get back to the student later.

SAY Now I'd like you to turn your index card over. Write a prayer in which you bring your concerns before God and thank him for the grace he gives you even when you have doubts or concerns.

Concerns

(recorded by Clear)

Standing in a sea of people—
So many voices,
Faces shaped by different stories,
So many choices.
From the pauper to the wealthy man,
From the high down to the low,
Does our star shine any brighter?
Everybody wants to know.

It concerns me—
Do I know you know my name in this crowded
    place?
Do I know you're not ashamed of my life's dis-
    graces?
Do you wash my sins away so I don't wear stains?
It concerns me.

Staring at this sea of people,
I hear them calling.
Each one seeking self-perfection—
I see them falling.
Did you really heal the dying man?
Did you really save his soul?
Could this God wash one like me?
Everybody wants to know.

I might as well be nameless,
The times I feel so small.
But all the love you sent is evidence
You see me standing tall.

And I know you know my name in this crowded
    place.
I know you're not ashamed of my life's disgraces.
You wash my sins away.
No, I don't wear stains.

Seeing Is Believing

Read John 20:24-25.

• About what sorts of things do you think, "I'll believe it when I see it"?

• What do you think made Thomas doubt the word of the disciples he knew so well?

• If you had been in Thomas' position, what do you think your reaction to the disciples' claim would have been?

Read John 20:26.

• Imagine you were there when Jesus came—literally—through the door. How do you think you would have felt?

• How would you have felt if you were Thomas?

Read John 20:27.

• Why do you think Jesus told Thomas to touch his wounds?

• What do you think Thomas' emotions were at that point?

Read John 20:28-29.

• What does Thomas' reaction tell you about Thomas? about Jesus?

• In what ways do you think it might be more "blessed" to be a believer who has not seen Jesus in the flesh?

• How do you feel about being one of the believers who has not seen Jesus?

Read John 20:30-31.

• What role has the Bible—the things "recorded in this book"—played in what you believe?

Read the Key Verse below. Using it and the story of Thomas, work together as a group to write your own answer to the question "What does it mean to have faith?" (Be sure to write your answer so you can share it with the other groups.)

> ### KEY VERSE
> "Now faith is being sure of what we hope for and certain of what we do not see" (Hebrews 11:1).

[t h i n k]

research required

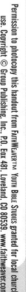

Taking It Home

take home [

everywhere

Driving Home the Point:

The disciples stand in a long line of doubters who grow into heroes of the faith. The whole Bible is full of doubts. The psalmists keep asking, "Hath God forgotten to be gracious?" Job complains that God is silent. Jeremiah asks boldly, "Wilt thou be to me like a deceitful brook?" As someone has said to Christian doubters, "The Bible is your book."

But the strange and wonderful thing is that God so often chooses doubt as his highway to Zion. God can turn even this desert into a fruitful field. **The sturdiest faith often comes out of doubt.**

So "Doubting Thomas" gasps out perhaps the shortest and most beautiful confession of faith in all the Bible: "My Lord and my God."

(Cornelius Plantinga Jr., **Beyond Doubt**)

Talking At Home:

Read Hebrews 4:14-16 with your family, and discuss these questions:

• **What encouragement can we find from these verses when we have doubts or struggles?**

• **What might it mean to hold firmly to our faith even while we're struggling?**

Ask each family member to describe a time he or she struggled with doubts. Ask if those doubts were ever resolved, and if so, how.

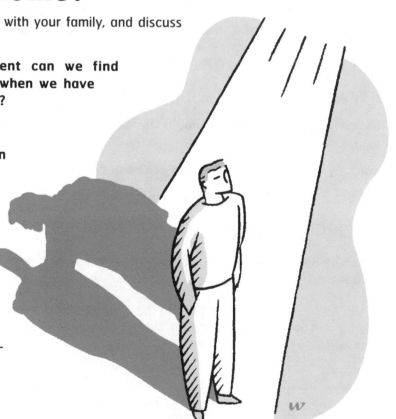

Key Verse:
"But the Counselor,
the Holy Spirit, whom the
Father will send in my name,
will teach you all things and
will remind you of
everything I have said to
you" (John 14:26).

A Look at the Study

Study Sequence	Minutes	What Students Will Do	Classroom Supplies
Getting Started	10 to 15	**Power Trip**—Discover invisible power in science experiments and compare that power to power from God.	"Power in Science" handouts (p. 96), scissors, plastic bowl, pepper, jar, water, liquid dish-detergent, balloons, empty aluminum cans, paper, pens
Bible Story Exploration	10 to 15	**Now Praying!**—Create advertisements for Pentecost.	Bibles, photocopies of "Historical Context" box (p. 91), newsprint, markers
	15 to 20	**First Power**—Discuss why God sent his Holy Spirit in the way he did.	Bibles
	15 to 20	**Power to Serve God**—Write devotions based on passages about the Holy Spirit.	Bibles, "Powerful Passages" handouts (p. 97), pens, newsprint, tape, markers
Bible Application	10 to 15	**Power to Connect**—Learn that just as electrical power is essential to running an appliance, so is the Holy Spirit's power essential to their ability to effectively serve God.	Bibles, blender, frozen orange juice concentrate, water, paper cups, index cards, tape, markers, power cords
	up to 5	**Faith Journal**—Respond in writing to the Key Question.	Index cards, pens
Music Connection	10 to 15	**Fill Me With Your Spirit**—Create a mural depicting people's lives that are directed by the Holy Spirit. Use this option at an appropriate time in the study.	CD: "Fill Me With Your Spirit" (Track 10), CD player, newsprint, markers

Age-Level Insight

There is much debate as to what the Holy Spirit does and doesn't do today. Teenagers can easily be caught up in the debate. Help your students navigate the various opinions by encouraging them to change their focus from *how* the Holy Spirit does things to *why* he does them. Remind teenagers that Jesus promised that "the Holy Spirit, whom the Father will send in my name, will teach you all things and will remind you of everything I have said to you" (John 14:26). By approaching the debate with an understanding of the Holy Spirit's primary purposes, teenagers will have a foundation for understanding the things the Holy Spirit may or may not do.

Getting Started

Power Trip

Before students arrive, set up two "science stations" by setting out the supplies listed on the "Power in Science" handout (p. 96). Cut apart the handout, and put each half at the appropriate station.

SAY **We're going to be talking about the power of the Holy Spirit today. To start, we'll be looking at some examples of power in science.**

Have students form two groups, and assign each group a science station. Allow groups about three minutes to conduct their experiments. Once group members have completed their experiments, have them write down the scientific principles they think were at work in the experiments. Then have groups switch stations.

When groups have tried both experiments, have everyone gather in the center of the meeting room.

SAY **Now that you've all had a chance to try the experiments, let's discuss the reasons you feel the experiments worked the way they did.**

Have groups read their explanations to everyone.

ASK • **What provided the power in each experiment? Explain.**

• **Could you see the power that made the balloon move the can? Or did you just see the effects of the power? Explain.**

• **How is the power in these experiments like God's power? How is it different?**

• **Does God give us power to do amazing things? What things does God expect us to do with his power?**

SAY **Today we're going to talk about God's power. More specifically, we're going to talk about the Holy Spirit, which God gave us so we could do powerful things. Let's begin by looking at how the Holy Spirit empowered the first disciples.**

Bible Story Exploration

Now Praying!

Have teenagers form groups of four. Give each group a Bible, a copy of the "Historical Context" box (p. 91), a sheet of newsprint, and colored markers or pencils.

SAY **With your group, I'd like you to read the "Historical Context" handout I've given you and the passage of Scripture it refers** to. Then create a poster advertising the Holy Spirit's coming at Pentecost. Your poster should be designed to draw people from the region to the big event.

Give groups an opportunity to share their posters.

ASK • **What do you find remarkable about the way the Holy Spirit came to the church?**

Historical Context | Acts 2:1-21; 3:12-19

Fifty days after the Passover celebration, the Jews celebrated the Feast of Weeks, otherwise known as Pentecost. However, the celebration described in this passage from Acts was a very special one. Jerusalem was crowded with Jews from many surrounding areas who had gathered in the holy city for the feast. Many of them spoke languages other than the Aramaic and Greek that were most common in Palestine at that time. God had set the stage for a miraculous display of his power through the Holy Spirit.

We could take a long time discussing the sound, the tongues of fire, and who was present for all this as described in Acts 2:1-3, but we would probably not gain much from the discussion. One can gain a basic understanding of it from reading the Bible text. What is important to glean from this passage is that the Holy Spirit came upon Christians in a new and powerful way, enabling them to better spread the good news about Jesus. They were filled with God's Holy Spirit.

We could also take a long time trying to sort out exactly what the term "speak in other tongues" (Acts 2:4) means, but instead we'll simply examine the event described in this passage. Somehow the disciples were able to speak so that people from several different ethnic groups could hear them in their own languages. Speaking in a language that the speaker had never learned does not necessarily mean that what is spoken is a message from God. We must remember that the Enemy is a great imitator. In this passage, however, we're given the evidence we need to verify God as the source of the message: The disciples were "declaring the wonders of God."

Why did some accuse the disciples of being drunk (Acts 2:13)? In every crowd there are doubters. When they heard uneducated men speaking in other languages, they concluded that their utterances must be nonsense. They hardened their hearts and missed out on a miracle!

Notice who takes the lead in verse 14 and the powerful message he gives. Could this be the same Peter who, only seven weeks earlier, had three times denied even knowing Jesus? the same Peter who had hidden with the other disciples behind locked doors for fear of the Jews? Indeed it is. Peter's experience with the risen Christ and the filling of the Holy Spirit made Peter a new man!

Peter had no delusions about the source of the power he exhibited. He readily pointed out that the crippled man (described in Acts 3:1-10) was not healed by any power of Peter's, but by the power of faith in Jesus.

God sent the Holy Spirit to empower his people to further his kingdom. Although Jesus had risen several weeks earlier and had spent time with the disciples after the resurrection, nothing is recorded in the Bible of any witnessing efforts prior to the events at Pentecost. In fact, Jesus had told his followers before he ascended to heaven that they were to wait in Jerusalem for the Holy Spirit to come upon them. God knew that they needed the power of the Holy Spirit to spread the good news.

We can learn an enormous lesson from this event: When God has something big for us to do for him, he'll empower us to do it. And he may use us in remarkable ways if we're willing to follow the leading of the Holy Spirit and let him work in our lives.

- **Why do you think the Holy Spirit arrived in such a way?**

- **How do you think Jesus' followers felt when the Holy Spirit arrived?**

- **How do you think the others felt?**

SAY God did not need flashy advertisements to introduce the Holy Spirit to the church. He sent his Spirit to demonstrate to the world that Jesus is the way to salvation.

First Power

SAY Understanding why God gave us the Holy Spirit is important. But let's first read about how the Holy Spirit was first introduced to Christ's followers.

Have students form four groups, and give each group a Bible. Have each group read Acts 2:1-15.

SAY This passage describes how the Holy Spirit first began giving people who believed in God the power they needed to do great things for God. I'm going to assign your group a passage, and I'd like you to create a "freeze-frame" sculpture to show the main idea of the passage. In your sculpture, the members of your group will act as the clay. Make sure all of the members of your group are involved in the sculpture. If your passage contains more than one main event, you may need to create more than one sculpture. You have five minutes to create your sculptures.

Assign one of the following passages to each group: Acts 2:1-4; Acts 2:5-12; Acts 2:13; and Acts 2:14-15.

When groups have finished, have groups present their sculptures in the order of the Bible story.

ASK • **What do you find interesting about the Holy Spirit's arrival?**

- **Why do you think the Holy Spirit's arrival was such a powerful moment? Explain.**

- **Does this passage give you any clues about why God gave us the Holy Spirit?**

SAY You did a great job of illustrating this passage. Now I'd like us to read a little further in the Bible—because there's more here. It's obvious that the Holy Spirit is powerful, and his entrance into our world certainly caused people to question the Holy Spirit's effect on others. But right after Peter stood up to address the men who were making fun of them, he said something that gives us a clear picture of why God gave us the Holy Spirit.

Have a volunteer read Acts 2:16-21 aloud.

ASK • What does it mean to prophesy and see visions?

• Do you think people prophesy and see visions today? Why or why not?

• Why did God give us the Holy Spirit?

Power to Serve God

SAY God's Holy Spirit gives us the power to serve God. We can serve God without his Holy Spirit, but we won't be truly effective. I'd like you to consider what it means to be used by the Holy Spirit. I'm going to give you a passage to read, and I'd like you to create a one-minute devotion about how God's Holy Spirit empowers us to serve him.

Have students form groups of four, and give each group a copy of the "Powerful Passages" handout (p. 97) and a pen. Have teenagers take on the following responsibilities in their groups: One person will be the writer, one person will be the speaker, and two people will be the researchers. Have groups work together to create and write their devotions based on the passages listed on the handout. When groups have finished, have them present their devotions to the whole group.

ASK • Based on what you've just heard, why did God give us the Holy Spirit?

• How should we respond to the Holy Spirit in our lives?

As students report their answers, write them on newsprint taped to the wall. When they've shared all their ideas, have students review the list.

SAY It's easy to think that God can use us only if we can speak well in public or have some other upfront ability. Actually, God wants to use us to do a variety of things, including those we've listed here.

Bible Application

Power to Connect

Before this activity, pour frozen orange juice concentrate and the appropriate amount of water into a blender.

SAY God has given us his Holy Spirit so that we can serve him. Serving God can feel like a huge task. But consider what we've studied today. We've seen people who simply did what God asked. In order to do what God asked, they had to be connected to God. I'd like to show you what I mean.

Point out the blender, and show students that the blender is unplugged. Point out that with the blender unplugged, the contents of the blender will settle and won't become orange juice. Then plug the blender in, and start it. Wait for the juice to finish mixing, then offer everyone a cup of juice.

SAY **The key to being empowered by God's Holy Spirit to serve him is staying connected to God. If we choose not to stay connected to God, we'll be spiritually slow and ineffective, like a blender without electricity. But if we stay committed to God and connected to him, he can use us to do mighty things through the power of his Holy Spirit. It's so easy to forget the importance of staying connected. But here's another awesome thing about God's Holy Spirit. I'd like to read it to you.**

Give each student a Bible, and read John 14:26 aloud together. Explain that God's Spirit doesn't just empower us, it also reminds us of everything that we know about God. Distribute a power cord, a piece of tape, a marker, and an index card to each student. Have each student write one thing on the card that he or she wants to commit to as a result of today's study. Encourage students to work today's Key Verse into their statements. For example, a student might write, "Lord, since you've promised to remind me of everything, please remind me to serve you this week." Students might want to commit to being more "in touch" with God or stepping out and trying to serve him more. Have students tape their cards to their power cords.

When students have finished, have them form a circle and bow their heads. Walk around the circle as you pray for strength and protection for each student as he or she attempts to serve God through the power of his Holy Spirit.

Faith Journal

Give each student an index card and a pen. Have teenagers write their answers to the following question on their index cards:

• Why is the Holy Spirit important to you?

After teenagers have written their responses, ask them to return the cards to you. Before you meet with the group again, take time to write personal responses to your students on their index cards. You may want to keep a notebook or a box containing copies of these index cards as well as brief notes of prayer concerns and needs your students share using this assessment tool.

For further information about the Faith Journal option, refer to page 5 of the Introduction.

Music Connection

idea:listen

Roll out a large sheet of newsprint and set out markers.

SAY **God sent his Holy Spirit to teach us and to give us power to serve him. I'm going to play a song by Big Tent Revival called "Fill Me With Your Spirit." This song demonstrates our need for the Holy Spirit.**

 Track 10
Play the song.

ASK • **What does this song say about the Holy Spirit?**

• **How can you tell if someone's life is directed by the Holy Spirit?**

SAY **Together with your classmates, I'd like you to create a mural depicting people's lives when they have the Holy Spirit. Work together to turn this sheet of newsprint into a mural showing the effects of the Holy Spirit on people and the world.** When students have finished, post the newsprint on a wall.

Fill Me With Your Spirit

(recorded by Big Tent Revival)

I remember clearly when I received your grace,
How I prayed sincerely as tears ran down my
    face.
The Spirit that you sent me to open up my eyes
Seems so very distant from this world of compro-
    mise.

Jesus, fill me with your Spirit, Lord.
Jesus, fill me with your Spirit, Lord.
Let all creation know that I have been restored.
Fill me with your Spirit, Lord.

Lord, I must confess my sinfulness and pride
And empty out this mess of ugliness inside.
Teach me true repentance; send your Spirit, Lord,
Until it's overflowing and there's room for noth-
    ing more.

I can live on nothing less than all your love and
    righteousness!
Jesus, fill me with your Spirit, Lord.
Fill me with your Spirit.

Permission to photocopy this handout from FaithWeaver™ Youth Bible Studies granted for local church use. Copyright © Group Publishing, Inc., P.O. Box 481, Loveland, CO 80539. www.faithweaver.com

Experiment 1: Scared Pepper

Materials needed: a plastic bowl, pepper, a jar of water, and liquid dish-detergent

Step 1: Pour some water into the bowl.

Step 2: Pour some pepper into the bowl of water

Step 3: Add one drop of liquid soap. What happens?

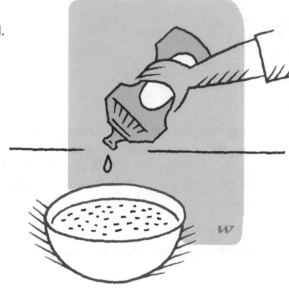

Experiment 2: Remote Control Roller

Materials needed: balloons and empty aluminum cans

Step 1: Put an aluminum can on its side on the floor.

Step 2: Blow up a balloon, and rub it on the back of your head really fast.

Step 3: Hold the balloon about an inch in front of the can.

Step 4: Move the balloon slowly away from the can. What happens?

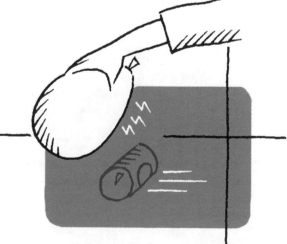

[think]

"I will not venture to speak of anything except what Christ has accomplished through me in leading the Gentiles to obey God by what I have said and done—by the power of signs and miracles, through the power of the Spirit. So from Jerusalem all the way around to Illyricum, I have fully proclaimed the gospel of Christ" (Romans 15:18-19).

"When the Counselor comes, whom I will send to you from the Father, the Spirit of truth who goes out from the Father, he will testify about me" (John 15:26).

"For it will not be you speaking, but the Spirit of your Father speaking through you" (Matthew 10:20).

"Because our gospel came to you not simply with words, but also with power, with the Holy Spirit and with deep conviction" (1 Thessalonians 1:5).

"To one there is given through the Spirit the message of wisdom, to another the message of knowledge by means of the same Spirit, to another faith by the same Spirit, to another gifts of healing by that one Spirit, to another miraculous powers, to another prophecy, to another distinguishing between spirits, to another speaking in different kinds of tongues, and to still another the interpretation of tongues. All these are the work of one and the same Spirit, and he gives them to each one, just as he determines" (1 Corinthians 12:8-11).

How to Create a Devotion

If you aren't sure just how to make your passage apply to the lives of others, use these questions to help you:

1. What's behind the passage? Who was the passage intended for? Why is the writer communicating this truth?

2. What's the main point of the passage?

3. What does the passage mean to you? How might you apply this passage to your life?

4. How can you apply this passage to the lives of others? What can you draw out of this passage that will help others live the truth that this passage contains?

Permission to photocopy this handout from FaithWeaver™ Youth Bible Studies granted for local church use. Copyright © Group Publishing, Inc., P.O. Box 481, Loveland, CO 80539. www.faithweaver.com

research required

take home everywhere

Driving Home the Point:

A.J. Gordon, one of the founders of Gordon Conwell Divinity School, told of being out walking and looking across a field at a house. There beside the house was what looked like a man pumping furiously at one of those hand pumps. As Gordon watched, the man continued to pump at a tremendous rate; he seemed absolutely tireless, pumping on and on, up and down, without ever slowing in the slightest, much less stopping.

Truly it was a remarkable sight, so Gordon started to walk toward it. As he got closer, he could see it was not a man at the pump, but a wooden figure painted to look like a man. The arm that was pumping so rapidly was hinged at the elbow and the hand was wired to the pump handle. The water was pouring forth, but not because the figure was pumping it. You see, it was an artesian well, and the water was pumping the man!

When you see a man who is at work for God and producing results, recognize that it is the Holy Spirit working through him, not the man's efforts that are giving results. All he has to do—and all you have to do—is keep your hand on the handle.

(Michael P. Green, editor, **Illustrations for Biblical Preaching**)

Talking At Home:

Read Acts 3:12-19 with your family, and discuss these questions:

• **How did Peter serve God in this passage?**

• **How did the Holy Spirit give Peter confidence to say what he needed to say?**

• **How can we do what Peter did?**

Ask family members to tell about times they served God and knew they made a difference. Ask each person if he or she felt "filled with the Holy Spirit" at that time.

OK to copy

Full On!

Acts 4:5-14

 key question: Why can we be courageous?

 study focus: Teenagers will examine how they can be courageous and discuss the things God might be able to do through them if they have courage.

> **Key Verse:**
> "Have I not commanded you? Be strong and courageous. Do not be terrified; do not be discouraged, for the Lord your God will be with you wherever you go" (JOSHUA 1:9).

A Look at the Study

Study Sequence	Minutes	What Students Will Do	Classroom Supplies
Getting Started	10 to 15	**No Fear**—Create stories about fear using a limited vocabulary.	Bible
Bible Story Exploration	10 to 15	**Same as It Ever Was**—List modern-day parallels to Peter and John's situation.	Bibles, pens, photocopies of "Historical Context" box (p. 101)
	15 to 20	**Going for the Gusto**—Discuss Acts 4:5-14 and learn about Peter and John's courage.	Bibles, "A World of Courage" handouts (p. 106), pens
	15 to 20	**Spontaneous Courage**—Act out various situations in which courage is required.	"Role Cubes" handouts (p. 107), scissors, tape
Bible Application	5 to 10	**What I Could Do!**—Commit to stepping out to do something for God using the courage he gives them.	Paper, envelopes, pens, index cards
	up to 5	**Faith Journal**—Respond in writing to a variation of the Key Question.	Index cards, pens
Music Connection	10 to 15	**In the Name**—Imagine battle royal match-ups between television characters or personalities while considering God's power. Use this option at an appropriate time in the study.	CD: "In the Name" (Track 11), CD player

Age-Level Insight

The illusion of invincibility gives adolescents a strong (although unfounded) sense of courage. Many teenagers will try just about anything (as long as it doesn't threaten their peers' perception of them). Help your teenagers see that they really are invincible when it comes to living for Christ. They may lose friends and popularity by taking a stand for Jesus, but they cannot be separated from the love of God. And the temporary pain and embarrassment are certainly worth the eternal reward.

As teenagers arrive, greet them warmly, and ask follow-up questions to review last week's study and Key Verse. Ask questions such as "Did you stay connected to God last week? Explain." and "How did your family members serve God last week?"

If you used the Faith Journal option last week, take this time to return your students' index cards to them.

Teacher SkillBuilder

Asking your teenagers to step out and try amazing things for God will produce interesting results. Be on the lookout for

• **failure.** Some students who step out and try things for God fail. Help them see that when they try to live courageously for God, they're never failures.

• **uncertainty.** Students might sit through this study and still have no idea of how God wants them to affect the world for him. Arm yourself with ideas to get these students thinking about what they can do in their own communities.

• **success.** Students who try to live courageously for God and are successful need shepherding. Lead them to a deeper understanding of what happened, and help them discover ways to repeat their successes.

Getting Started

No Fear

Have students form groups of three or four.

SAY **To begin today's study, I'd like us to do a little experiment. We're going to try an exercise in fear. First, I'd like you to tell the other members of your group one thing you're afraid of.**

Give group members a few minutes to share their fears. Then have volunteers share with the whole group.

SAY **Great job. Now I'd like you to share one way to deal with your fears. Ready? Go!**

Allow group members to discuss how to deal with fears, then have volunteers share their discussions with the entire group.

SAY **OK, now for the experiment. I'd like each group to come forward, one at a time. Members of a group will stand shoulder to shoulder in a line and then follow my directions exactly.**

Have the first group come forward and line up. To the rest of the class,

SAY **For this experiment to work, I'll need you all to stop talking. Thanks.**

To the group standing in the front of the class,

SAY **I'd like each of you to imagine that your vocabulary is limited to three words at a time. Your task is to create a short story about someone who is afraid and how he or she conquers the fear. But since each of you has a vocabulary of only three words at a time, you'll have to begin and continue the story with each person sharing only three words. Here's an example of how this might work. The first person might say, "One day, Jimmy"; the second person might say, "went out to"; and the third person might say, "clean the car." The story would then continue from there. First group, are you ready to create your story for us? Go!**

Have each group create its story in front of the class in turn. When all the groups have finished,

ASK • **Who here is afraid of public speaking? Why?**

• **Were you a little afraid when I asked you to do this? Why?**

• **How might your fears have been eased?**

• **What part does being courageous play in this type of exercise?**

• **When are some other times you've had to be courageous?**

• **Where does courage come from?**

Read Joshua 1:9 aloud.

SAY The Bible talks a lot about people who did amazing things for God—all because they stepped out and took chances with God's guidance and help. Today you'll see that God used these people when they understood that God wanted them to take chances and have courage.

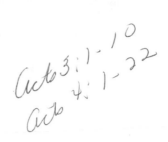

Historical Context | Acts 4:5-14

In this passage, Peter and John are called before the elders and teachers of the Law to explain the healing of the disabled man described in Acts 3:1-10. This group of Jewish leaders (the Sanhedrin) was the ruling body of the Jews. It had authority in all religious matters and in certain legal matters granted to it by the Romans. One of the Sanhedrin's duties was to pronounce judgment in cases of blasphemy. Members of the Sanhedrin probably viewed Peter's and John's actions as bordering on blasphemy. Peter and John claimed that they were able to heal a man—something only God could do—through the power of Jesus, who the Jews contended was dead. So they called Peter and John before them to hear the explanation firsthand.

When asked the source of his power to heal, Peter replied that the power came from Jesus and accused the Jewish leaders of crucifying Jesus, whom God then raised from the dead. The Jewish leaders were intent on getting rid of Jesus, but God nullified their actions by raising him from the dead. The Sanhedrin had tried to cover up the Resurrection (Matthew 28:11-15), but Peter contended that the healed man standing before them proved that Jesus is alive.

Notice that the disabled man was healed through Jesus' power and that Peter's forceful speech before this powerful group of religious leaders was made possible by the power of the Holy Spirit (Acts 4:8). God was with Peter in a special way, as Jesus had promised he would be when people were going about his work (Matthew 28:20).

Why didn't the Sanhedrin immediately denounce Peter and John? Perhaps the truth, told with such power, dumbfounded them—or even convicted them of what they really had done. And Peter hadn't finished yet!

In verse 12, Peter indirectly heaps on more accusation. By saying that salvation is only through Jesus, Peter was saying that all of the Jewish leaders' beliefs and actions were insufficient. He was saying that if they continued to deny Jesus, no other power was available to save them. He was saying that if they continued along this course, they were not only destroying themselves, but they were also leading their nation toward destruction.

What was the Sanhedrin's response? Astonishment! How could these simple men, with no training in the Jewish rabbinical schools, mount such a clear and convincing biblical and theological argument? The Jews' only answer was that "these men had been with Jesus"! They may have remembered the similar things they had thought about Jesus (John 7:15). Jesus had supported his claims through the miracles he had performed, and now the disciples had done the same. Everyone had seen the disabled man begging at the Temple, and now he stood before them, healed. What could they say? The Sanhedrin had no answer.

At least two things gave Peter courage in this intimidating situation. First, he was relying on the Holy Spirit, and second, he knew beyond the shadow of a doubt that Jesus is alive. This knowledge gave Peter full and ultimate trust in Jesus. We have the apostles' (and God's!) record in the Bible, and we have the same Holy Spirit that empowered Peter. What more do we need to be courageous in the situations we face today?

for **Younger**
teenagers

Have younger teenagers act out the passage, write first-person narratives from Peter's and John's perspectives, or create clay sculptures to represent Peter's and John's thoughts and feelings during this incident.

Bible Story Exploration

Same as It Ever Was

Have students form groups of four. Give each student a Bible, a photocopy of the "Historical Context" box (p. 101), and a pen. Have students read Acts 4:5-14 and their handouts, then have each group think of modern-day situations in which Christians have or may experience similar situations. For example, groups could list the persecution of Christians in some countries in the Middle East or standing up for Christ in their schools.

Allow groups to share their lists.

ASK
- **How is courage necessary to Christians around the world today?**

- **How do Christians in our area need to demonstrate courage?**

- **How is this like or unlike the courage Peter and John demonstrated?**

Going for the Gusto

Give each student a "World of Courage" handout (p. 106), a pen, and a Bible. Have students form pairs, and assign each pair one of the following sets of characters: Peter and John, the religious leaders, and the crippled man and his family. Have pairs read Acts 4:5-14 again and respond to the questions on their handouts from the perspectives of the roles they've been assigned. When pairs have finished discussing, have them form groups with the other pairs who were assigned the same roles. Once groups have discussed their answers, have each original pair get together with one pair from each of the other perspectives (you'll have groups of six). Have groups share their answers with one another. When groups have finished, read each question aloud, and have volunteers share their answers.

ASK
- **What did you discover about courage by studying this passage? Explain.**

- **If you could write a definition of courage based on what you've just read and discussed, what would it be?**

- **How does courage help us to do great things for God?**

- **Does God want us to be courageous? Why?**

- **Why can we be courageous?**

SAY
The point of this passage is that God used these two men. They made themselves available to God, and he gave them the courage they needed to do great things for God. God hasn't stopped using people to do his work. He desperately wants to use us—if we'll let him. Have you ever stopped to think about how God might use you if you had the courage to surrender to him? I'd like us to explore what might happen if we took the chance and let God use us.

For Extra **Impact**

If you really want to help students understand courage from a modern perspective, use the following clip from *The Truman Show*. First explain to students that Truman has spent his whole life in a make-believe world, but he really wants to learn about the real world. Show the movie from the point where Truman fights the storm through the end. Ask students to describe the type of courage it takes to conquer the seemingly impossible, the scary, or the undiscovered things in this world. Help students to understand that when we rely on God, we can do things for him that may seem impossible.

Spontaneous Courage

Before this activity, create two "Role Cubes" using the handout on page 107.

SAY **We've discussed two people in the Bible who had great courage and did awesome things for God because of it.**

ASK • **How can you have courage?**

• **Why do you need courage?**

Have students form pairs. Explain that each pair will roll both cubes then act out the roles that land face-up. The "situation" cube will tell the two actors what is going on, and the "emotion" cube will stipulate an emotion the actor responding to the situation will display. For example, if the situation cube lands on "One of you would like to tell the other why you don't do drugs," and the emotion cube lands on "anger," the pair could act out an argument in which one actor feels judged by the actor who is explaining his or her reasons for not doing drugs.

Ask one pair to volunteer to go first. Then give all the pairs a chance to do a role-play.

ASK • **What part did the characters' emotions play in the outcome of each role-play?**

• **How do others' emotions affect our courage in standing up for God?**

• **What does it take to be courageous?**

• **Why do we need courage?**

Bible Application

What I Could Do!

SAY **Courage is a gift from God, but it's not a selective gift. God doesn't give courage to just a few chosen people. Whoever chooses to step out to do great things for God is given the courage to do it. What do you want to do for God?**

Ask students to close their eyes and dream about the things that they could do for God. Ask them not to limit themselves by what people have told them they can or can't do; encourage them to dream a little bigger.

Give each student a piece of paper and a pen.

SAY **I'd like you to describe your dream in writing. Write a letter to yourself that begins with the following statement: "Dear Me, I have a dream to…" Take as much room and time as you need.**

After students have written their letters,

ASK • **How can the Holy Spirit help you turn this dream into reality?**

for OLDER teenagers

Older teenagers might want to approach this activity a bit differently. Have them form trios and talk about times they tried to do great things for God but failed because they lacked courage. Then read the Key Verse again, and encourage students to talk about how God's courage might help them the next time they have a chance to do great things for him.

Tip From the Trenches

The impromptu nature of this activity might make some of your students uncomfortable. The activity is intentionally unstructured to help your students really think about the emotions surrounding courageousness. If you think your students' discomfort might hinder their ability to act out the roles, you may want to write some of your own roles before the meeting.

Tip From the Trenches

You may want to play some soft, reflective music during this activity.

• How can courage from God help you?

SAY As with Peter and John, when we dream of doing awesome things for God, his Holy Spirit gives us the courage to turn those dreams into reality. Now I'd like you to commit to fulfilling your dream by reading your letter to yourself a few times.

When students have finished, have volunteers share their letters. Then give each student an envelope, and have students address the envelopes to themselves. Tell students that you'll be mailing their letters to them in thirty days. Give everyone an index card, and ask students to write a short version of their dreams on the cards. Encourage teenagers to place the cards in their Bibles and read the cards several times during the next week.

SAY We all want to do something awesome and powerful for God. I don't know what you dream of doing for God, but I know God's response to those who want to be used by him to do great things. Let me read it to you.

Read Joshua 1:9 to students. Ask students to listen to the verse as you read it again and then paraphrase the verse on the back of their index cards. When students have finished,

SAY I'll be praying for you as you attempt to fulfill the dream you described in your letter.

Tell students that when they get their letters in the mail, they're to evaluate their courage in stepping out and doing great things for God.

Faith Journal

Give each student an index card and a pen. Have teenagers write their answers to the following question on their index cards:

• How can you use the courage that comes to you through the Holy Spirit?

After teenagers have written their responses, ask them to return the cards to you. Before you meet with the group again, take time to write personal responses to your students on their index cards. You may want to keep a notebook or a box containing copies of these index cards as well as brief notes of prayer concerns and needs your students share using this assessment tool.

For further information about the Faith Journal option, refer to page 5 of the Introduction.

Tip From
the Trenches

To help strengthen the connection between church and home, photocopy the "Taking It Home" page at the end of this study, and either distribute copies to students before they leave or mail them to their homes. Encourage students to complete the reading, activities, and discussion with their families during the coming week.

Music Connection

idea:listen

[music]

Have teenagers form pairs.

SAY With your partner, I'd like you to think up the ultimate battle royal. You can pick any two famous people for the battle. For example, you could choose to have The Nanny fight Steve Urkel or have Pokémon go head-to-head with Barney. After you've chosen the participants, decide who would win the fight and why. Please avoid any offensive material.

Allow pairs to share their battles.

SAY You've demonstrated some, um, amazing powers. However, God would win over all of the participants combined. God is the most powerful force in the universe. The great news is that he's here to help you. I'm going to play a song by Jennifer Knapp called "In the Name." As you listen, think of all the things, other than God, that people consider powerful or put their trust in.

Track 11
Play the song.

ASK • What does it mean to trust in the name of the Lord our God?

   • Do you trust in God's name? Why or why not?

   • How have you seen God come through for you in your life?

In the Name

(recorded by Jennifer Knapp)

All these years, too many ahead to think clear.
Some say, "Where's my crystal ball?"
Some men play the lottery, makin' bets against
   the government's economy.
They say, "I'd rather be rich than be alive at all."
When men in miry circumstances fall,
It won't be hard to tell where they place their
   resolve.

Some trust in chariots,
But we trust in the name of the Lord our God.
"To each his own" won't lead you home;
It probably never will.

Picket fences may build up our defenses
In domestic wars of leisure suits.
That's OK; it doesn't bother me.
You can hold on to your philosophy.
What's mine is mine; what's yours is yours,
But what's the truth?

When the walls do crumble and they fall,
It won't be hard to tell where we place our resolve.

I won't trust in the things I do
'Cause they will not stand, and they won't come
   through.
So I'll trust in the name of the Lord my God.
I will trust in the name.

When the walls do crumble,
What will I find to hold onto that's stronger than
   my Jesus?
Sing hallelujah, hallelujah...
When the walls do crumble and they fall
No, it won't be hard to tell where we place our
   resolve...

A World of Courage

[think]

research
required

Permission to photocopy this handout from FaithWeaver™ Youth Bible Studies granted for local church use. Copyright © Group Publishing, Inc., P.O. Box 481, Loveland, CO 80539. www.faithweaver.com

• **Why did the religious leaders arrest Peter and John?**

_____

_____

• **Why didn't they recognize the source of the power that Peter and John displayed?**

_____

_____

• **Why did God want Peter and John to be courageous?**

_____

_____

• **Would you have been able to say to the religious leaders what Peter said? Why or why not?**

_____

_____

• **Why didn't the religious leaders do something horrible to these two men?**

_____

_____

• **What does this passage tell you about courage?**

_____

_____

• **How did God give these two men courage?**

_____

_____

• **What did these two men accomplish because of their courage?**

_____

_____

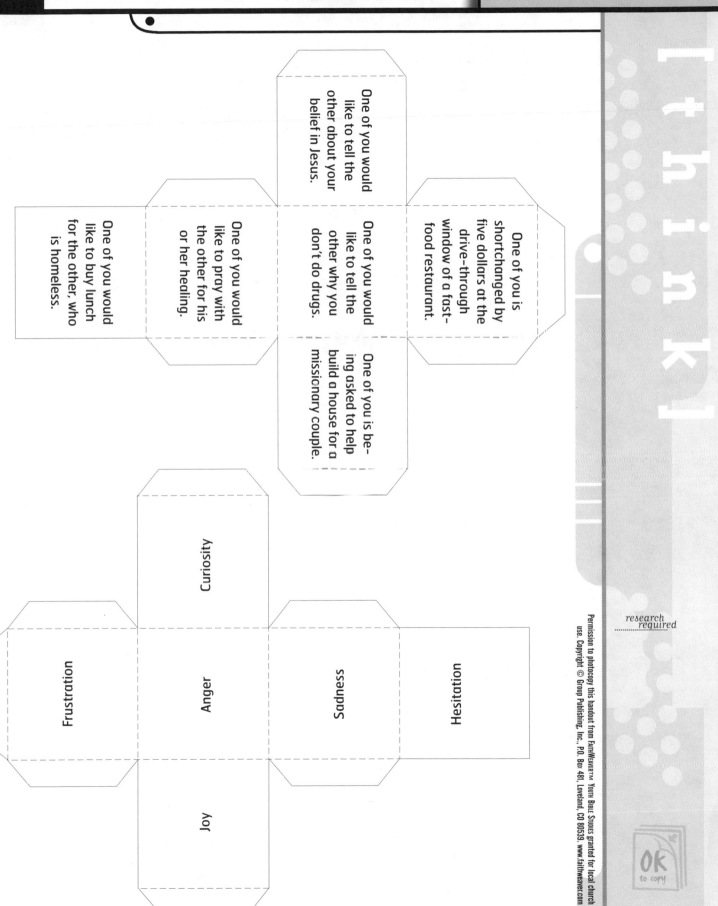

One of you would like to tell the other about your belief in Jesus.

One of you is shortchanged by five dollars at the drive-through window of a fast-food restaurant.

One of you would like to tell the other why you don't do drugs.

One of you would like to pray with the other for his or her healing.

One of you would like to buy lunch for the other, who is homeless.

One of you is be-ing asked to help build a house for a missionary couple.

Curiosity

Frustration

Anger

Sadness

Hesitation

Joy

research required

Permission to photocopy this handout from FaithWeaver™ Youth Bible Studies granted for local church use. Copyright © Group Publishing, Inc., P.O. Box 481, Loveland, CO 80539. www.faithweaver.com

OK to copy

Talking About It

Driving Home the Point:

British Antarctic explorer Sir Ernest Shackleton...placed this advertisement in London newspapers in 1900 in preparation for the National Antarctic Expedition (which subsequently failed to reach the South Pole)...

"Men wanted for hazardous journey. Small wages, bitter cold, long months of complete darkness, constant danger, safe return doubtful. Honor and recognition in case of success."

(William J. Bennett, **The Book of Virtues**)

Talking At Home:

Read Philippians 1:27—2:4 with your family, and discuss these questions:

• **Would you answer an ad like the one above? Why?**

• **Does it take courage to try things that other people are afraid to do? Explain.**

• **How can we have courage in the midst of suffering?**

• **What things do we need to do as a family that might take the type of courage that God promises?**

Ask each family member to share a time he or she used God-given courage to accomplish something awesome. Ask how it felt and how family members might advise others who would love to have that type of courage.

Straight Paths

Acts 8:26-40

12

Philip Tells the Ethiopian About Jesus

 key question: How should we respond to God's leading?

study focus: Teenagers will explore how to determine where God is leading them.

Key Verse:
"But the Fruit of the Spirit is love, joy, peace, patience, kindness, goodness, faithfulness, gentleness and self-control. Against such things there is no law" (GALATIANS 5:22-23).

Study Sequence	Minutes	What Students Will Do	Classroom Supplies
Getting Started	15 to 20	**Mixed Messages**—Experience the limits of their own understanding.	"Your Own Understanding" handouts (p. 115), scissors
Bible Story Exploration	10 to 15	**What If?**—Consider what might have happened if Philip had disobeyed.	Photocopies of "Historical Context" box (p. 111), Bibles, pens
	20 to 25	**When God Leads**—Add sound effects to a reading of the story of Philip and the Ethiopian and create children's books about God's leading.	Bibles, paper, newsprint, markers, tape
Bible Application	10 to 15	**Fruits That Follow**—Spend time in personal reflection about where God is leading them.	Bibles, "Fruits That Follow" handouts (p. 116), pens
	up to 5	**Faith Journal**—Respond in writing to the Key Question.	Index cards, pens
Music Connection	10 to 15	**What Would Jesus Do?**—Come up with phrases like "What would Jesus do?" to demonstrate how to live out their faith. Use this option at an appropriate time in the study.	CD: "What Would Jesus Do" (Track 12), CD player, card stock, markers

Age-Level Insight

Junior highers are still trying to understand if and how God leads them. They are learning to make decisions and just beginning to see that they can rely on God to help them with those decisions. Senior highers are more concerned with what God is leading them to do. They understand that they will soon make some important life choices and are eager to experience God's leading in those choices. As you explore this study with your students, consider sharing stories from your life that illustrate how God has led you, what he has led you to do, and the results of your obedience.

Last Week's Impact

As teenagers arrive, greet them warmly, and ask follow-up questions to review last week's study and Key Verse. Ask questions such as "How did you use God's courage in your life this week?" and "How did the members of your family experience God's courage?"

If you used the Faith Journal option last week, take this time to return your students' index cards to them.

Teacher SkillBuilder

Don't be surprised if your students struggle with the questions in this activity. The goal is to help them see how far their own limited understanding actually takes them. Some trios may not come up with any answers, and they may want to give up. Many teenagers are used to understanding things pretty easily, but struggling with a difficult challenge can be good for them and can teach them not to give up when they struggle to understand God. So in this activity, control your urge to help them understand or give them hints.

Getting Started

Mixed Messages

Before class, cut apart the "Your Own Understanding" handout (p. 115), and set the answers aside. If you have more than nine students in your class, you'll need to make more than one copy of the handout.

Have students form trios. Distribute one question from the "Your Own Understanding" handout to each trio.

SAY **Work together in your trio to figure out the correct answer to your question. There's only one correct answer to each question. You'll have five minutes to discuss the question and come up with your answer.**

After five minutes, see how many trios have the correct answers to their questions. Then ask the trios to discuss the following questions and share their answers with the entire group after each one.

ASK • **What happened in your trio during this exercise?**

• **What information did you need in order to figure out the answer?**

• **How was this exercise like or unlike the way we try to determine where God is leading us?**

SAY **There are many things in life that we may have a hard time understanding. Let's take a few moments to think of those things. When you think of a concept that's difficult to understand, just shout it out. For example, I really don't understand why life isn't fair to everyone.**

Give students a few minutes to share ideas.

ASK • **In general, how do you feel about things you don't understand?**

Bible Story Exploration

What If?

Give each teenager a Bible, a copy of the "Historical Context" box (p. 111) and a pen.

SAY **I'd like you to read the Scripture passage listed on the handout I've just given you. Then read the handout. On the back of the handout, describe in writing how the story would have turned out if Philip had told God he was too tired or busy to talk with the Ethiopian. Then think about the consequences of Philip's imagined disobedience in a**

Philip was a deacon, chosen by the apostles to help with ministry in the early church. He had gone to Samaria and established a wonderful ministry there. According to Acts 8:4-8, Philip was preaching Christ, healing people, and bringing great joy to a Samaritan city. But God had another plan for Philip, which included guiding the first non-Jew to faith in Jesus and resulted in Christianity being taken to Ethiopia. Philip responded in obedience.

Since the Ethiopian eunuch had gone to Jerusalem to worship, we can assume he knew something of the Jewish faith. He may have been quite fully committed to the faith because he had traveled quite a distance to worship, perhaps as far as two hundred miles! He had likely been inspired by his time of worship, because he was reading from Isaiah as he rode along. We might find it strange that Philip could hear what he was reading, but it was common in ancient times to read aloud. In fact, the language was such that sounding out the words was almost necessary.

Notice that at the Holy Spirit's prompting, Philip overcame not only any fears or questions about non-Jews becoming Christians, but also any racial prejudice he may have had. The Ethiopian was a native of Africa and therefore was black-skinned. God is not concerned with the color of our skin, and neither was Philip.

Philip had no difficulty answering the Ethiopian's questions. He had probably been answering the same types of questions from the Samaritans. God had prepared the right person to present the gospel to the Ethiopian on the road.

When Philip told the man about Jesus, the Ethiopian apparently expressed belief immediately. Baptism was taken very seriously in the early church. Philip must have been fully convinced of the certainty and sincerity of the Ethiopian's belief, because he consented to baptize this traveler.

Having completed his task, Philip was again sent on his way by God. The text seems to indicate that God miraculously swept him away, on to his next mission. The Ethiopian continued on his way, and tradition tells us that he spread the message of Christ in Ethiopia, soon baptizing the queen and others there.

We often don't know why God guides us to do certain things. Sometimes what he leads us to do seems difficult, even illogical. But when we know what God wants us to do, we must respond in faith and action. Philip's actions opened Christianity to non-Jews, and if we accept tradition as true, they also resulted in many Ethiopians following Christ. Who knows what God will do through us if we respond faithfully to the guidance of his Holy Spirit?

larger context, and consider how the region and maybe even the world would have been different.

After they've written their ideas, allow students to share their thoughts.

SAY **It is vitally important for us to follow God's leading. We never know what will result from our obedience or disobedience. God may lead you to reach out to another student at your school. Maybe your actions will prevent a tragedy that student would have been involved in. Maybe that person will become the next Billy Graham. We must follow God's leading because his plans and reasons are much bigger than we understand.**

When God Leads

Before this activity, write the following questions and incomplete sentences on a sheet of newsprint. Post the newsprint where students can see it.

- Page 1: How had the Ethiopian been exposed to God in the first place? (See verse 27.) To determine where God is leading us, we begin by...

- Page 2: What was the Ethiopian doing to understand what God wanted him to do? (See verse 28.) To determine where God is leading us, we need to...

- Page 3: Who did God send to help? (See verses 29-33.) To determine where God is leading us, we need to find...

- Page 4: What did Philip do to help? (See verses 34-35.) To determine where God is leading us, we need...

- Page 5: How did the Ethiopian respond? (See verses 36-38.) How can we respond to God's leading?

SAY **Because there are so many things in our lives that we don't understand, we need to trust God's promise to lead us. It may not always be clear to us where or how God is leading us, but we know we can trust God to lead us in the right direction. Let's read the story about Philip and the Ethiopian again. As the story is read, interrupt by making the sound of a loud buzzer every time you hear any hint of anyone being led by God in any way.**

Have a volunteer read Acts 8:26-40 aloud. Each time students make the sound of a buzzer, have the reader pause as you

ASK • **How do you perceive God's leading?**

• **Does God lead people in this way today? Explain.**

• **What would you have done if you were in that person's shoes?**

SAY **This story not only shows us how to follow God's leading, but it also gives us a step-by-step process for determining how we can respond to that leading.**

Have your students form trios, and give each trio a Bible, two sheets of paper, and markers. Show trios how to fold the paper in half horizontally to make booklets. Direct trios' attention to the information on the newsprint, and ask them to use it to create a children's book about "determining where God is leading you and me." The booklets should contain a title page and a simple illustration and sentence on each page. Encourage trios to be as creative as possible in creating their booklets.

When trios have finished, have them share their booklets with the entire group.

ASK • **How can we determine if God is leading us?**

• **What makes it difficult to know how God is leading us?**

• **How should we respond to God's leading?**

Bible Application

Fruits That Follow

Ask each student to move to a position where he or she can spend the next several minutes working alone. Then give each student a "Fruits That Follow" handout (p. 116). Give students a few minutes to complete the questions on their handouts.

SAY **One way to determine if God is leading you to do something is to think about the fruit it will produce. If following will lead you to the fruit of the Spirit, there's a good chance God is directing you to follow.**

Have your students form pairs, and encourage them to share the problems they just reflected on and their current plans of action. Have each pair designate a Partner 1 and a Partner 2, and then close by having the whole group say the "Fruit Litany" printed on the handout.

Faith Journal

Give each student an index card and a pen. Have teenagers write their answers to the following question on their index cards:

• **How can you respond to God's leading in your life?**

After teenagers have written their responses, ask them to return the cards to you. Before you meet with the group again, take time to write personal responses to your students on their index cards. You may want to keep a notebook or a box containing copies of these index cards as well as brief notes of prayer concerns and needs your students share using this assessment tool.

For further information about the Faith Journal option, refer to page 5 of the Introduction.

Tip From the **Trenches**

To help teenagers get into a more reflective mood, you may want to play soothing, quiet, background music.

Tip From the **Trenches**

To help strengthen the connection between church and home, photocopy the "Taking It Home" page at the end of this study, and either distribute copies to students before they leave or mail them to their homes. Encourage students to complete the reading, activities, and discussion with their families during the coming week.

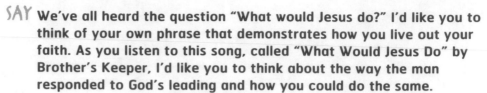

SAY We've all heard the question "What would Jesus do?" I'd like you to think of your own phrase that demonstrates how you live out your faith. As you listen to this song, called "What Would Jesus Do" by Brother's Keeper, I'd like you to think about the way the man responded to God's leading and how you could do the same.

Track 12
Play the song.

Have students form pairs, and give each person a piece of card stock and markers.

SAY Together with your partner, create your own slogan to describe the way you live out your faith. If you'd like, you can use the letters WWJD to stand for other words, or you can come up with your own acronym. Write your slogan on the card stock, and decorate it as you'd like.

When students have finished, ask them to share their slogans. Encourage students to take the slogans with them and to put them where they'll see the slogans often.

What Would Jesus Do

(recorded by Brother's Keeper)

I met a man of faith; he taught the way of truth—
A giant among men, from my point of view.
He said that life lies in front of you;
Finding the path is in how you choose.

Quiet your noisy heart; listen from your knees.
There'll be a tiny voice: "What would Jesus do?"

He spoke of trying times, of learning how to
   choose,
Finding healing love when your heart is bruised.
Someone will be watching over you;
He will speak out when you need him to.

Whispering softly, the wind has a voice
Asking you what would he do.

I met a man of faith; he taught the way of truth—
A giant among men, from my point of view.

Quiet your noisy heart; listen from your knees.
There'll be a tiny voice whispering, "What would
   Jesus do?"

From the album *Brother's Keeper*. Words and music by D. Key and P. Eber-sold. Copyright © 1999 Ardent/Koala (ASCAP) and Frankly Scarlett Music, Memphis Southern Music (BMI). All rights reserved. Used by permission.

Question 1: There is a grandfather clock that chimes the appropriate number of times to indicate the hour, as well as chiming once at each quarter hour. If you were in the other room and heard the clock chime just once, what would be the longest period of time you would have to wait in order to be certain of the correct time? (The clock is working properly and is set at the correct time.)

CUT

Answer 1: You would have to wait ninety minutes between 12:15 and 1:45. Once you had heard seven single chimes, you would know that the next chime would be two chimes for two o'clock.

CUT

Question 2: What is the next figure or symbol in the following sequence?

CUT

Answer 2: The next figure or symbol is ⊢. The sequence is the letters A to E. The right half of each figure is the letter, and the left half is its mirror image.

CUT

Question 3: A man, his wife, and their two sons come to a river they wish to cross. They find a rowboat on the riverbank; however, the boat can carry a maximum of 150 pounds at a time. Both the man and woman weigh 145 pounds each. Their sons each weigh 75 pounds. How will they get across the river using the boat, and how many trips will it take?

CUT

Answer 3: It will take five round trips.

1. The two boys cross together, and one comes back.

2. The mother rows across, and the boy who was waiting alone rows back.

3. The two boys cross together again. One stays with his mother, and the other rows back to his waiting father.

4. The father rows across and joins his wife. The boy who was waiting with his mother then rows back to where his brother is waiting.

5. The two boys row back and join their parents.

CUT

(Questions and answers from the game Mind Trap)

Fruits That Follow

Take some time to sort out how God has been leading you. Think of a situation in your life that you're not sure how to handle.

• My situation or question:_____
_____
_____

• In what ways have you looked for God's guidance lately?_____
_____

• Read Galatians 5:22-23 in your Bible. What does this passage say to you about your situation?
_____
_____

• How can one or more of the fruits of the Spirit come out of your situation?_____
_____

• What specific people has God given you to help you with your situation?_____
_____

• What do you think God wants you to do?_____
_____

• How can you respond to your situation?_____
_____

Fruit Litany

All: "But the fruit of the Spirit is

Partner 1: love,

Partner 2: joy,

Partner 1: peace,

Partner 2: patience,

Partner 1: kindness,

Partner 2: goodness,

Partner 1: faithfulness,

Partner 2: gentleness and

Partner 1: self-control.

All: Against such things there is no law."

research
required

Driving Home the Point:

"Nowhere in the Bible does it say that God is going to give you a plan for your entire life. He never said that He would lay out His plan for your life in cinemascope so you can view it in its entirety. What He does promise is to lead you as you go; to direct you day by day; to show you His will hour by hour."

(Tony Campolo, **You Can Make a Difference**)

Talking At Home:

Read Psalm 139:9-10 with your family, and discuss these questions:

• **How might the words in these verses make it easier to understand God's plan? to follow it?**

• **In what ways have you seen evidence of God's plans for your life already?**

Use the thought starters below to help family members share stories of how God has brought them to where they are today.

• **Things I liked to do as I grew up:**

• **Things I like to do now:**

• **People who have had a significant influence on my life:**

• **How those people influenced what I am doing today:**

• **Doors that were closed to me:**

• **Doors that opened for me:**

• **Significant spiritual experiences:**

• **How my faith has grown:**

Permission to photocopy this handout from FaithWeaver™ Youth Bible Studies granted for local church use. Copyright © Group Publishing, Inc., P.O. Box 481, Loveland, CO 80539. www.faithweaver.com

everywhere   [take home]

OK to copy

Lord of All

Acts 10:1-44

13

 key question: Who should we tell about Jesus?

 study focus: Teenagers will examine their openness to sharing Christ with everyone.

Key Verse:
"Therefore go and make disciples of all nations, baptizing them in the name of the Father and of the Son and of the Holy Spirit, and teaching them to obey everything I have commanded you. And surely I am with you always, to the very end of the age" (Matthew 28:19-20).

A Look at the Study

Study Sequence	Minutes	What Students Will Do	Classroom Supplies
Getting Started	10 to 15	**Who Do You Hang Around?**—Discuss how they decide who to associate with. **What Will You Do?**—Imagine relating to different people in school.	Newsprint, markers, tape
Bible Story Exploration	10 to 15 15 to 20	**Overcoming Barriers**—List the barriers Peter overcame to join Cornelius. **The Turning Point**—Create mime scenes to illustrate Acts 10:1-44.	Bibles, photocopies of "Historical Context" box (p. 122), pens Bibles, "The Turning Point" handouts (p. 127), scissors, pens, newsprint, markers, tape
Bible Application	15 to 20 up to 5 up to 5	**Stretch Me, O Lord**—Make rubber band bracelets. **Faith Journal**—Respond in writing to the Key Question. **Quarter Review**—Reflect on what they've learned during the past thirteen studies.	Newsprint, tape, wide rubber bands, permanent markers Index cards, pens Newsprint, tape, markers
Music Connection	10 to 15	**Truth About God**—Individually create a song, poem, or statement that describes especially meaningful aspects of their faith. Use this option at an appropriate time in the study.	CD: "Truth About God" (Track 13), CD player, paper, pencils

Age-Level Insight

At this stage in their development, teenagers have the verbal skills to communicate their beliefs to their friends. However, few teenagers actually tell their friends about their faith. As you explore this study with your students, consider using it as a springboard to encourage them to tell others about Jesus. After this study, you might want to organize an outreach event to give your students an opportunity to share their faith.

As teenagers arrive, greet them warmly, and ask follow-up questions to review last week's study and Key Verse. Ask questions such as "How has God helped you to follow his leading?" and "What experiences about following God did the members of your family share?"

If you used the Faith Journal option last week, take this time to return your students' index cards to them.

Younger teenagers may have a hard time quickly verbalizing their choices in friendships. To help them think this through, you may want them to list their three closest friends and list the similarities they see among the three.

Getting Started

Who Do You Hang Around?

Write the following sentence stems on a sheet of newsprint, and post it on the wall for your students to see as they enter your meeting room.

• I usually don't hang around kids who...

• I mostly hang around kids who...

Have students find partners, and have each pair decide which partner will speak first. Have each student choose a sentence stem to finish, then give pairs about thirty seconds to finish their sentences. Then have students form new pairs, and have them finish the sentences again. Continue in this manner until each person has had the opportunity to talk to everyone else.

ASK • **How do you choose who to hang around with? Explain.**

• **What did you learn by talking with each person here today?**

• **What kinds of things get in the way of building relationships with other people?**

• **How do those same things affect our ability to share our faith with other people?**

• **Who should we tell about Jesus?**

Who would you go to = a ? @ your faith?
Who would you like to share something @ your faith with?

What Will You Do?

SAY **Sit back, close your eyes, and listen carefully as you imagine yourself in the following situation.**

Read the following scenario to students, pausing as indicated to give them time to envision the scene you're describing.

SAY **Imagine yourself entering your school's cafeteria. You are standing just inside the doors that you usually use to enter the cafeteria. See yourself standing there, and carefully look all around the room. Think about the way the tables are arranged, and imagine the food lines. (Pause.) Now imagine the room is filled with people. Think about the noise in a crowded cafeteria. (Pause.) Think of the wide variety of people who attend your school.**

Now imagine your friends sitting at one of the tables. Make sure you take time to think about each of their faces. (Pause.) Imagine what they are doing as they are sitting there (pause), what they are wearing (pause), and what they are talking about (pause).

Now, at a different table, imagine another group of people you don't really know. They're people you don't hang around with, but they could be your friends. You've just never gotten to know them. Think about their faces. Who are they? (Pause.) What do they look like? (Pause.) Imagine leaving your friends

and sitting down with these other students for lunch. Imagine what that might feel like. (Pause.) Now think about your friends' reactions to what you just did. What are your friends saying about you? (Pause.)

Now imagine another table. You would never hang around with the people at this table—they make very different choices from yours. Who are these people? What do they look like? What are they wearing? What are they talking about? (Pause.) Now imagine one of them is coming over to talk to you. You're still sitting there in the cafeteria with all of your friends, and this person comes over to ask you to eat lunch with him or her. (Pause.) You never hang around with people like this. What would you do? (Pause.)

Ask a few volunteers to share their thoughts and feelings about what they would think and do in each of the situations you described.

SAY We're blessed with friends—people who are gifts from God to us. These people help us and care for us and share life with us. Yet those friendships sometimes keep us from opening ourselves to others who are different from us.

ASK • How can the people you hang around with affect your ability to open up to others?

• Who do you think God wants you to hang around with?

• Who should we tell about Jesus? ❓

Bible Story Exploration

Overcoming Barriers

Give each teenager a Bible and a copy of the "Historical Context" box (p. 122). Form trios, and give each trio a pen.

SAY I'd like you to read the Scripture passage listed on the handout. Then, with your trio, read the handout. As you read, list all of the barriers Peter had to overcome to join Cornelius. List the barriers mentioned in the handout as well as other barriers you can imagine, such as the reaction of Peter's own family.

Have trios share their lists.

ASK • What barriers do you face in sharing Jesus with others?

• How can you overcome those barriers?

Historical Context | Acts 10:1-44

This passage begins at the home of Cornelius, a Roman centurion in Caesarea, the headquarters for the Roman occupation of that area. As a centurion, Cornelius would have been in charge of a unit of about one hundred men and would have been considered a man of noble character. For a non-Jew to have been considered God-fearing meant that Cornelius followed the Jewish religion to some degree, possibly to the greatest extent he could as a non-Jew. His vision of the angel at about three in the afternoon likely means that he was following Jewish religious practices since that was a regular time of prayer for the Jews. And it is to his credit that when an angel of God spoke to him, he didn't hesitate to do what he was told.

Today one might question the validity of building a theology on dreams and visions. However, dreams and visions such as that experienced by Peter in this passage were a common means God used to deliver his messages to people during Bible times. Though God may still speak to us in unusual ways, we have the Bible as his primary means of communication and as a guide for determining the validity of any of those unusual modes of communication.

Peter's vision came to him as he was praying at noon—another of the regular times of prayer for Jews. Peter, too, was following normal Jewish religious practices. Another of these practices was the strict adherence to the dietary restrictions spelled out in Leviticus 11. Many of the forbidden animals described there were included in the sheet suspended before Peter in his vision. Being told to kill and eat such animals shocked Peter.

Peter's response was reminiscent of his rebuke of Jesus when he talked about his own coming death (Mark 8:31-33). Jesus in turn rebuked him, as God here rebuked Peter for not immediately responding in belief. And then the whole scene was repeated twice to fully convince Peter of its validity. We don't know if Peter refused to believe the first two times or if God simply repeated the vision for the sake of absolute confirmation. God uses such threefold repetitions throughout the Bible to greatly emphasize a point.

The challenge to Peter's beliefs didn't end when the sheet disappeared. It was obviously no coincidence that Cornelius' servants appeared just as Peter's vision ended. Peter was thinking through the meaning of his vision when he was summoned to go to the house of a non-Jew who said an angel had told him to send for Peter to hear what he had to say. And God made it clear to Peter that the servants' arrival was connected to what God was trying to teach him. God told him that the men were there, that he had sent them, and that Peter was to go with them. It became apparent to Peter that the vision had much wider implications than the food Christians were to eat.

By the time he arrived at Cornelius' house, Peter had apparently sorted out the meaning of his vision. Though Jewish regulations forbade him to enter a non-Jew's home (as he himself states in Acts 10:28), Peter went right inside with Cornelius and many other non-Jews gathered there.

Peter's proclamation in Acts 10:34-35 seems logical and appropriate to us now, but it stunned the non-Jews gathered there and possibly revolted the Jews who had come with Peter. Considering non-Jews to be fully accepted by God was a new concept for Jews, who believed that their status as "chosen people" granted them special favor before God.

Peter took a huge risk in following God's leading to reach out to Cornelius and his family. The Jewish Christians were likely appalled by his actions. In fact, when he returned to Jerusalem, he had to explain his actions and describe how God had directed them. Only then did the Christians there open their hearts to allow that non-Jews could become Christians (Acts 11:1-18).

Peter set an example for us by taking advantage of an opportunity to tell someone unexpected about his faith. We dare not ignore that example; rather, we must be willing to tell anyone who is interested about what God has done for us through Jesus.

The Turning Point

Before class, photocopy the "Turning Point" handout (p. 127), and cut apart the sections. (If you have more than ten students, you'll need more than one copy of the handout.) Have students form pairs, and give each pair Bibles, a section of the handout, and a pen.

SAY **First I'd like you and your partner to read your assigned section of the Bible story and then answer the questions on the handout to help you understand the story. Then I'd like you to create a mime scene to illustrate the action that takes place in your part of the story. You have ten minutes to do this.**

Give pairs ten minutes to study the Scripture and plan their scenes, then have students report on each section. As pairs are reporting, write the highlights of their insights on a sheet of newsprint, then post it on the wall. This will give you an overview of the entire story to refer to. Then have pairs mime their scenes to the rest of the class, in order.

SAY **The events in this story represent an important turning point for the church.**

ASK • **What if this event had never happened?**

   • **What would the church look like today?**

   • **What would people think about Jesus?**

Have students form new pairs, and give each pair a sheet of newsprint and markers.

SAY **In your new pair, I'd like you to describe or draw a picture of what our world or the church would look like now if Peter and Cornelius had not acted on the Spirit's urging.**

When pairs have finished, have them share their creations with the class.

ASK • **How important were Peter's and Cornelius' actions to the church then and now?**

   • **How would Peter and Cornelius have answered the question "Who should we tell about Jesus?"**

> ## for OLDER teenagers
>
> If the older teenagers in your group would rather not create mime scenes, have pairs describe what happened in their sections of the story instead of acting the events out.

Bible Application

Stretch Me, O Lord

Before this activity, write the following words from the Key Verse in large letters on a sheet of newsprint, and post it on the wall: "Therefore go and make disciples of all nations."

SAY **The "what if" questions extend to us, too.**

ASK • **What if we aren't willing to share our faith with people who are different from us? What will happen to the church?**

Give each student a wide rubber band, and set out several permanent markers.

SAY **Christ is the Lord of *all* people. We need to stretch ourselves to constantly reach out to others, even those who aren't like us.**

ASK • **Who do we need to tell about Jesus?**

SAY **Now I'd like each of you to choose one word of the Key Verse to write on your rubber band. Think about which word best indicates how you need to stretch yourself in order to reach out to others. For example, if you have an easy time making friends with all different kinds of people but a hard time helping people grow in faith, you might choose the word "disciple" to write on your rubber band.**

Give students a minute to do this.

ASK • **Who do you personally need to tell about Jesus?**

SAY **I'd like you to think of one or two people who are very different from you. You would really have to "stretch" to include these people in your life. These might be people you imagined in the cafeteria scenario earlier. Write their names on the inside of your rubber band.**

Give students a minute to do this.

SAY **I'd like you to take your rubber band with you this week and wear it on your wrist. When you see it, it will remind you to stretch yourself to share your faith with others.**

Finally, join your students in a time of prayer. Ask them to include the names of people they could make more of an effort to include in their lives. Have each person complete this sentence prayer: "Stretch me, Lord, to be open to _____ and _____." If students would rather keep the names private, let them pray silently.

Faith Journal

Give each student an index card and a pen. Have teenagers write their answers to the following questions on their index cards:

• **Who should you tell about Jesus? How can you do that?**

After teenagers have written their responses, ask them to return the cards to you. Before you meet with the group again, take time to write personal responses to your students on their index cards. You may want to keep a notebook or a box containing copies of these index cards as well as brief notes of prayer concerns and needs your students share using this assessment tool.

For further information about the Faith Journal option, refer to page 5 of the Introduction.

Quarter Review

Write the following statements on newsprint, and post the newsprint where students can see it.

• My favorite lesson this quarter was...

• One thing I've learned that has affected me is...

• I plan to share what I've learned by...

Have students form pairs and take turns finishing the statements in their pairs. When they've finished sharing, have volunteers share their answers with the whole group.

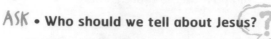
ASK • Who should we tell about Jesus?

• What should we tell people about Jesus?

• How should we tell people about Jesus?

SAY I'd like to play a song for you called "Truth About God," by All Together Separate. It's about a man who has found Jesus. As you listen, think about how you might tell someone about your faith.

Track 13
Play the song. Give each student a piece of paper and a pencil.

SAY Now I'd like each of you to write a poem, song, or statement that describes what you have found in your faith.

When students have finished, have a few volunteers share their writings.

SAY Take what you have written with you, and remember what it says. The next time you're presented with an opportunity to tell someone about Jesus, use what you wrote to help you.

Truth About God

(recorded by All Together Separate)

I found the answers you need.
Are you listening?
I'll tell you the truth about God.
My eyes haven't seen him;
These hands never touched him.
I've never seen the wind,
But I felt the breeze today.
I don't know where it came from,
And I don't know where it went.
But this kite can't deny it's in the sky.

Just like a lost man
Stumbling through the scorching sand,
With flashes and mirages all around.
The sun is going down,
And everything he's found
Has left him further out than when he began.

Bloody are his fingers,
And sweat drips from his brow.
He's got it in his mind

By digging deeper, he will find
Satisfaction in the sand dripping from his hands.
But you don't hear me.

The Turning Point

Study 13 ....

1. Cornelius' vision in Caesarea (Acts 10:1-8)

• What happened?

• Use three words to describe Cornelius.

• What could Cornelius have been feeling?

Create a mime scene (acting without talking) to demonstrate what happened.

CUT
- -

2. Peter's vision (Acts 10:9-16)

• What happened?

• Use three words to describe Peter.

• What could Peter have been feeling?

• How did Peter respond?

Create a mime scene (acting without talking) to demonstrate what happened.

CUT
- -

3. Cornelius' messengers come to Peter (Acts 10:17-23a)

• What happened?

• Use three words to describe Peter.

• What could Peter have been feeling?

• How did he respond?

Create a mime scene (acting without talking) to demonstrate what happened.

CUT
- -

4. Peter goes to Cornelius (Acts 10:23b-33)

• What happened?

• Use three words to describe Peter or Cornelius.

• What could Peter and Cornelius have been feeling?

• How did they respond?

Create a mime scene (acting without talking) to demonstrate what happened.

CUT
- -

5. Peter's speech (Acts 10:34-44)

• What happened?

• Use three words to describe Peter.

• What could Peter have been feeling?

• How did he respond?

Create a mime scene (acting without talking) to demonstrate what happened.

research required

[think]

Taking It Home

[take home] everywhere

Driving Home the Point:

Sarah and her parents fight all the time, and it all seems to revolve around Sarah's friends. Sarah has always chosen to hang around people who are, well, different. They aren't cheerleaders or student council representatives; they aren't the kinds of teenagers that Sarah's mom and dad were in high school. Sarah's friends are kind of "artsy"; they go to coffeehouses and create local trends. Sarah has always gravitated toward ideas, clothes, and activities that are different and creative.

Her parents always encouraged her creativity when she was younger. But now it scares them. They're pretty sure that some of Sarah's friends are involved in risky and unhealthy things. Sarah keeps reassuring her parents that she doesn't do that kind of stuff, but she wants to be able to hang around people she finds interesting. "And besides," she says, "how can I share my faith if I'm only hanging around people who believe exactly as I do?"

And so the battles continue. Sarah says her parents don't trust her. Her parents say they do trust her—it's her friends they don't trust.

Talking At Home:

Read Galatians 3:26-29 with your family, and discuss these questions:

• **What should Sarah do?**

• **What should her parents do?**

• **How could you handle these issues at your house?**

• **How could the Scripture help?**

Spend time in prayer with the members of your family, asking God to give you the strength to reach out to those who need Christ's love and the ability to trust God as he guides your outreach efforts.

OK to copy